Daytime Television Game Shows and the Celebration of Merchandise

Daytime Television Game Shows and The Celebration of Merchandise:

The Price is Right

Morris B. Holbrook

Bowling Green State University Popular Press
Bowling Green, Ohio 43403

Television and Culture
Robert Thompson, series editor

Copyright ©1993 by Bowling Green State University Popular Press

Library of Congress Catalogue Card No.: 92-75573

ISBN: 0-87972-620-2 Clothbound
0-87972-621-0 Paperback

Cover design by Gary Dumm

For

Sally,

Chris,

May,

Sandy,

and Skeptics Everywhere

Morris B. Holbrook is the W.T. Dillard Professor of Marketing, Graduate

School of Business, Columbia University, New York, NY 10027 (212-854-

3481).
The author gratefully acknowledges the support of the Columbia

Business School's Faculty Research Fund.

Americans have made a religion out of things (materialism) and, more
importantly,...they try to use "things" to express their search for the
meaning of existence

— Kilbourne (1987),
226-227.

Contents

Chapter 1
Introduction

This book applies an interpretive perspective to the neglected phenomenon of daytime television game shows in general and *The Price is Right* in particular.

In Part 1, Chapter 2 begins with some background on the development of studies in popular culture. The discussion turns in Chapter 3 to a comparison of the older leftist views (emphasizing the dominant ideological hegemony) with the more recent pluralistic cultural studies (stressing the role of resistant, negotiated, or oppositional readings). Next, Chapter 4 advances a proposition that—whatever the merits of the emerging pluralistic perspective—*The Price is Right* aspires to and largely achieves the status of a closed, readerly, univocal, monosemic text that demands a dominant reading strategy. Part 1 then concludes, in Chapter 5, with some revelations concerning the author's historically based personal biases against quiz or game shows and with a statement of reasons for the focus of the present study.

Part 2 turns its attention to the phenomenon of game shows in general. Chapter 6 reviews the different types of knowledge tapped by the various contemporary game shows. Chapter 7 focuses on their relation to the culture of consumption.

In Part 3, the focus narrows to a close reading of *The Price is Right* itself — the structure and imagery of its text, its materialistic subtext, and its commercial intertext. Specifically, Chapter 8 emphasizes the program's orientation toward the celebration of merchandise. Chapter 9 describes its structure of games and prizes. Chapter 10 characterizes its

1

studio audience of potential contestants and participants. Chapter 11 draws a portrait of its Master of Ceremonies, Bob Barker. Chapter 12 depicts the role in *The Price is Right* of merchandise on display. Chapter 13 presents an account of the "agonistics"—that is, the series of contests — involved in the show. Finally, Chapter 14 embraces a broader view of the commercial intertext surrounding the products advertised to the audience of television viewers who watch *The Price is Right*.

Part 4 gives full consideration to a competing interpretation of *The Price is Right*. Chapter 15 presents the resistant reading proposed by John Fiske. However, contra this Fiskean interpretation, Chapter 16 provides empirical evidence—based on data compiled over 31 broadcasts during the summer of 1991—to support a dominant reading of this particular game show from the viewpoint of hegemony theory as a closed, readerly, univocal, monosemic text. Specifically, this chapter includes a statistical analysis of the bidding behavior by contestants as a potential demonstration of the consumer expertise, shopping skills, or knowledge about product prices assumed as a key premise underlying the resistant reading suggested by Fiske. The empirical results indicate an absence of any real expertise, skill, or knowledge displayed by participants in *The Price Is Right*.

In Part 5, Chapter 17 presents a detailed interpretive analysis that compares *The Price Is Right* with another game show, *Supermarket Sweep*, in terms of a set of revealing structural homologies. This comparison reinforces the impression from earlier chapters that, whatever the relative esthetic and ethical merits of the two programs, daytime game shows in general and *The Price Is Right* in particular may be regarded as an expression of the capitalist ideology associated with a consumer culture in which the Ethos of Consumption requires sustenance and support via televised ritualistic ceremonies.

After a brief epilogue or envoi in Chapter 18 of Part 6, an

extended list of references appears in Part 7. Examination of these references will suggest that—compared with other facets of American television (say, soap operas, situation comedies, or news programs)—game shows have received rather sparse coverage. This book pursues the hope of inspiring wider interest in the phenomena of game shows in general and *The Price Is Right* in particular as windows on the fondness with which our Culture of Consumption regards the Celebration of Merchandise.

Part 1

Background

Chapter 2
From the Condemnation of Kitsch
to the Probing of Popular Culture

Contra Kitsch

Once upon a time—say, in the period of cultural criticism that covered the 300 years from about 1650 to about 1950—those who viewed themselves as the guardians of what Matthew Arnold called "Sweetness and Light" or "the best that has been thought and said" maintained strong barriers and demarcations between the realm of High Art (dedicated to the communication of beauty, truth, and wisdom) and the sphere of popular culture (aimed at the lowly tastes of the intellectually disadvantaged hoi polloi). Somewhat ironically, this division of cultural tastes into the higher- and lower-brow—the artistic and the popular—appeared on both sides of the otherwise unbreachable rift between the political left and the patrician right. (For reviews, see Fishwick; Fiske, *Introduction*; Fowles; Huyssen; Kaplan, "Introduction"; Modleski, "Introduction.")

Thus, from the right, authors such as T. S. Eliot, F. R. Leavis, Ortega y Gasset, and (maybe most vociferously) Dwight Macdonald concerned themselves with preserving the cultural tradition and argued relentlessly for the superiority of serious art against the debasement of taste evinced by kitsch or other symptoms of "masscult":

The market for cultural products has steadily broadened until by now practically everybody is a customer.... Now that the masses—that is, everybody—are getting into the act and making the scene, the problem of vulgarization has become acute. (Macdonald ix-x)

7

Meanwhile, from the Marxist left, members of the Frankfurt School such as Horkheimer, Benjamin, Adorno, and Marcuse contended that mass-produced ersatz culture aimed at the hoard of workers and other common folk simply perpetuated class conflicts via its ability "to reconcile its consumers to the status quo, thus serving the interests of capitalism" (Modleski, "Introduction" ix) by means of "ideological distortion" based on "a world of appearances which deceive people" (Larrain 15) so that "by giving people certain ideas, it is possible for the wealthy, who benefit most from the social arrangements in a capitalist country, to maintain the status quo" (Berger 36):

The most frequent theme in Marxist cultural criticism is the way the prevalent mode of production and the ideology of the ruling class in any society dominate every phase of culture.... This domination is perpetuated...through the often unconscious absorption of capitalistic values by creators and consumers in all the above aspects of the culture of everyday life. (Lazere 766; quoted by Berger 37)

(For reviews, see Berger; Boddy; Gendron; Larrain; Tetzlaff; White; Williamson.)

In sum, from both ends of the political spectrum, the attitude toward popular culture was essentially the same - unequivocal condemnation or what Fowles calls "Media Snobbery" (27, 79, 81) associated with "H. L. Mencken's dictum that no one ever went broke underestimating the intelligence of the American public" (70). This attitude lingers in the scorn that some commentators still direct at the television medium:

While music, magazines, books, fashions, and radio, with their multiple distribution channels and relatively low production costs per unit, can become the fetishes, pleasures, and identity badges of specific publics and subcultures, high-cost television with its vast profits automatically caters to a hypothetical least common denominator—or dips below it. (Gitlin, *Inside Prime Time* 30)

Thus, one encounters such epithets for television as "chewing gum for the eyes" (Fishwick 50), "garbage" (Fowles 75), "cultural junk food" (Rapping 6), "junk food for the mind" (Gitlin, *Inside Prime Time* 16; Berger 128), "mind candy" (Gitlin, *Inside Prime Time* 273), and "popcorn for the mind" (DeLong 234).

Pro Pop

More recently, however, a trend has appeared toward taking popular culture seriously as the legitimate manifestation of a particular type of taste. Expressed most conspicuously in the work of Herbert Gans, the view of democratically inspired sociologists now leans (sometimes with a rather precarious balance) in the direction of interpreting popular and high cultures—entertainment and art—as "separate but equal." (For a more recent update focused specifically on the case of television, see Fowles.)

This stance, of course, raises the perplexing question: "Equal in *what*?" If hard-pressed, we might reach some consensus on the proposition that the "equality" at stake applies to the capacity of different tastes to serve as windows onto the meanings attached to cultural artifacts by the citizens who appreciate them. Thus, considerable interest has focused on interpreting a wide range of consumer products including such otherwise humble artifacts as Coke bottles, postage stamps, television sets, and coal tipples (Browne and Fishwick) or television commercials, Big Macs, neon signs, comics, supermarkets, The Superbowl, and Walt Whitman as well as Walt Disney (Fishwick).

Masterman credits Barthes in *Mythologies* with the recognition that "a plate of steak and chips, a margarine advertisement and a poem were...equally worthy of serious attention"(1). Based on this premise, Schroeder adopts as the "essence of popular aesthetics" the principle that "if the product sells, it is good art; if it does not, it is bad art" (2). Schroeder then proceeds to direct his sustained critical attention toward pop songs (11), professional wrestling (34), mail-order catalogs (50), elementary school primers (62), cheap religious icons (149), and the American garden (94) with its

concrete, metal, ceramic and plastic reproductions of classical, Renaissance and oriental statuary: putti, urns, gazing balls and stone-lanterns...plastic ducks and ducklings for the lawn...sleek Virgin Marys, fiberglass fountains, ceramic frogs...Birdhouses, miniature windmills, animals, nursery-rhyme figures, religious grottoes and "planters" of all kinds...variously made of wood, spring metal, tin cans, bleach bottles, tires, bathtubs, beerkegs and toilets. (107)

In a similar vein, Huyssen suggests that "one of the few widely agreed upon features of postmodernism is its attempt to negotiate forms of high art with certain forms and genres of mass culture and the culture of everyday life" (203). Indeed, in describing "Postmodernism and Consumer Society," Jameson notes "the effacement...of some key boundaries or separations, most notably the erosion of the older distinction between high culture and so-called mass or popular culture" ("Postmodernism" 112). Jameson follows with a list of postmodernistic fascinations that includes

that whole landscape of advertising and motels, of the Las Vegas strip, of the late show and Grade-B Hollywood film, of so-called paraliterature with its airport paperback categories of the gothic and the romance, the popular biography, the murder mystery and the science fiction or fantasy novel. (112)

In short, I take it as a fundamental tenet in the emerging sociological and critical movement toward the study of popular culture that no aspect of the media, the marketplace, or the world of material objects is too lowly to offer a potentially advantageous vantage point commanding a view on the vistas of meaning available to the modern mind.

Indeed, it often seems that the lowliest—the most mundane, trivial, or vulgar—of social artifacts appear the most illuminating in terms of the light they shed on the meanings embedded in human culture.

Segue to the Game Show

In this spirit, I can imagine no artifacts of popular culture more apparently worthless and more seemingly unredeemed by any vestige of intellectual, esthetic, or moral value than those that constitute the daily spectacle paraded before the public in the form of television game shows. Indeed, though in the midst of a lengthy and learned disquisition on the subject of "Nonfiction TV," Rapping cannot resist pausing to single out game shows as "the dregs of American culture and American life itself" with the comment that "there is nothing in our culture which seems quite so embarrassing as these public displays of greed, misery, emotional excess and freakishness" (61).

As early as the late 1940s, Fred Allen charged that "give-away programs...are the buzzards of radio" (qtd. by DeLong 117). Today, Fiske calls TV game shows "the lowest form of television" ("Women and Quiz Shows" 134). On a similar theme, Hickey notes that "professional TV critics almost unanimously pronounce game shows the most primitive and banal form of televised entertainment"(66). As if on cue, the television critic for *The New York Times* describes the game show as a format in which "vacuity joins unashamed greed" (Corry C26), while a master of cultural studies takes time out to characterize *The Price Is Right* as "hardly...an intelligent show" (Gitlin, *Inside Prime Time* 50).

Inspired by these clarion calls, the present essay reports its author's interpretation of TV game shows in general and of *The Price Is Right*—that paragon of programmed paltriness—in particular.

Chapter 3
The Drift of Cultural Studies:
From Hegemony to Resistance

An interest in the game show leads us to the center of concerns addressed by a relatively new body of work on cultural studies of television. Here, we find ourselves plunged into a debate that has sprung up between the old left-leaning views handed down by various Marxists and a newer, more pluralistic perspective associated with the more recent cultural critics from Manchester.

Hegemony

Briefly, the older perspective—associated with the work of Gramsci, Althusser, or Barthes and exemplified in some of the writing on television by Williams (*Television*) or Gitlin (*Whole World* and *Inside Prime Time*)—tends to regard what appears on the tube as an exercise in the hegemony of a dominant ideology. (For reviews, see Brown, "Introduction"; Chambers; Fiske, "British," *Television Culture*, *Introduction*; Good; Gottdiener; Jhally, "Political Economy"; Larrain; Marchetti; Masterman; Press, *Women Watching*; Tetzlaff; White.) For example, Tetzlaff summarizes such "left theories of communication" as follows:

The key analytical term here is 'dominant ideology.' The ruling forces of society work to secure their position (consciously or unconsciously) by spreading an ideology that favors their interest, which becomes masked as nature or common sense. Mass-produced culture, of course, is a key agent in the reproduction of this ideological unification. (10)

As noted by Good, "critical" communication studies that pursue this perspective tend to focus on the locus of social power: "In fact, a 'critical' approach to communication is critical largely because it assumes that social relations of communication are inseparable from social relations of power" (52). In this connection, Good borrows from Gramsci's theory of "consent" (60) and views "hegemony" as posing "the problem of how...consensus is produced and who produces it" (61).

Jhally adds that "all societies seek to *reproduce* their constitutive social relations over time" and that "for...capitalism, ...the vital questions of reproduction concern how a minority but dominant social class (capitalists) can maintain power over the vast majority of the population": "Reproduction can be accomplished through the *consent* of the dominated.... In this the media are vital institutions" (*Political Economy* 67). Thus, Jhally summarizes, as follows:

In one very important variant of critical communications theory the function of the media and the cultural realm in general is to produce the appropriate *consciousness* in the majority of people to ensure the reproduction of what is essentially an exploitative system of social relations. Hans Enzenberger coined the phrase "Consciousness Industry" to describe the media.... The media here are literally an industry which attempts to produce a form of consciousness in the audience that benefits the class that controls the media and industry in general. (68)

Along similar lines, the account offered by White merits quotation as a nicely compact summary:

Ideological criticism is based on the assumption that cultural artifacts...express and promote values, beliefs, and ideas that are pertinent to the contexts in which they are produced, distributed, and received.... ideology refers to ideas, values, and beliefs that may be carried by...television programs. The cultural artifacts...are seen as reflecting the interests of the dominant class. For example, television...would necessarily reflect the belief system, the ideology, of the dominant class. Viewers are then seen as buying into this belief system.... A rather simple version of classical Marxism, applied to television, might argue that...television...instills bourgeois values. Thus...working class viewers exist in a state of false consciousness.... they are dupes of ideology....

Gramsci used the term *hegemony* to explain the complex ways in which the dominant class maintains control over society.... the ruling class exercises hegemony in that their interests are accepted as the prevailing ones...recognized as the prevailing common-sense view.... A more thoroughgoing reformulation of ideology was developed by...Althusser.... a text-oriented ideological criticism...examines television as an ideological practice—that is, as a complex system of representation through which individuals experie..ce and understand their world.... This more recent ideological criticism is concerned with the ways in which a particular text or group of texts functions as a part of ideological practice and offers a system of knowledge or a way of experiencing the world for a viewer. (136-142, passim)

As noted by Jameson, the *"société de consommation"* or "moment of...consumer or multinational capitalism" (*Political Unconscious* 11) calls for an *"ideological analysis"* aimed at "ideological unmasking" (12) so that "the political interpretation of...texts" becomes "the absolute horizon of all reading and all interpretation" (17). Toward this end (drawing principally on literary examples), Jameson develops the concept of *The Political Unconscious* viewed as "the repressed and buried reality" to be uncovered by "the unmasking of cultural artifacts as socially symbolic acts" (20). Drawing on Althusser, Jameson pays some attention to the problem of seeking a *unified meaning* amidst the "host of clashing and contradictory elements" to be found in a cultural artifact: "Althusserian exegesis...requires the fragments, the incommensurable levels, the heterogeneous impulses, or the text to be once again related...in the concept of totality" (56-57). Here, the unifying impetus—modeled, in part, on the psychoanalytic method (61)—views interpretation as a sort of ideological unmasking or demystification in which "interpretation proper...always presupposes...some mechanism of mystification or repression in terms of which it would make sense to seek a latent meaning behind a manifest one" (60). From this perspective, "the relationship between ideology and cultural texts or artifacts" resides in the premise that "the aesthetic act is itself ideological" (79). Hence, "the corrosive and tradition-annihilating...money and market economy...necessarily informs all of our cultural artifacts, from the literary institutions of high modernism all the way to the products of mass culture" (79-80). In this ideological *subtext* (81), amidst "those narrative unities of a socially symbolic type...designated as ideologemes" (185), one finds such ugly aspects of the capitalist ethos as "sexism and the patriarchal" (99), "commodity lust" (159), "the heroic bureaucracy of imperial capitalism" (265), and "the most degraded of all mass cultural texts, advertising slogans" (287)—to pick a few Marxist-inspired examples, more or less at random. Thus, though Jameson also holds out some hope for a more Utopian aspect of culture grounded in universal human values and collective unity, he summarizes the "negative hermeneutic function" (291) of the "Marxist analysis of culture" (291) in which the "manipulated viewer is offered specific gratifications in return for his or her consent to passivity" (287) as one of management and defusion: "The ideological function of mass culture is...a complex strategy of rhetorical persuasion in which substantial incentives are offered for ideological adherence" (287). Ultimately, Jameson ends by "reasserting the unidimensional power of ideological distortion that persists...within the...meaning of cultural artifacts" and by "reminding us that within the symbolic power of art and culture the will to domination perseveres intact" (299).

In this light, television becomes a vehicle for foisting the values of capitalism on the impressionable masses who uncritically absorb the domestic family-oriented implications of the sitcoms, the patriarchal thrust of the cop shows, the imperialistic ethos of the news programs, and (most of all) the materialistic mania of the commercials en route to being socialized into the prevailing norms of the consumer culture that serves as a fertile ground exploited by the capitalistic captains of consciousness. In the words of Mellencamp, "US television...appeals to an ideology of familialism (and happy cleanliness), to a myth of the middle-class, happy family reproduced in sitcoms, local news staffs, the *Today* show" ("Prologue" 11). According to Fiske, "This analysis...implies that the wide variety of codes all cohere to present a unified set of meanings that work to maintain, legitimate, and naturalize the dominant ideology of patriarchal capitalism" (*Television Culture* 13).

In an earlier work, Fiske and Hartley viewed television as performing a "bardic" role:

It seems, then, that television functions as a social ritual, overriding individual distinctions, in which our culture engages in order to communicate with its collective self.... we have coined the idea of television as our own culture's *bard* (85).... the classically conceived bard...composes out of the available linguistic resources of the culture a series of consciously structured messages which serve to communicate to the members of that culture a confirming, reinforcing version of themselves (85-86).... The bardic mediator tends to articulate the negotiated central concerns of its culture...with a predominance of messages which propagate and re-present the dominant class ideology. (89)

From this perspective, any individual TV program or indeed television as a whole—via what Williams calls its "flow"—serves as a text that indoctrinates its viewers into the dominant hegemonic ideology. Thus, in this view, a particular television show tends to serve as a "closed text" (Eco), a "readerly text" (Barthes), or a "univocal text" (Ricoeur) in the sense that it permits only one viable interpretation or what Hall calls a "dominant" reading strategy.

One sustained illustration of the hegemonic perspective inherited from Gramsci and the other aforementioned sources appears in a study of the mass media by Gitlin, who argues that "the mass media have become core systems for the distribution of ideology" (*The Whole World* 2) so that "television entertainment is...an ideological field" (18). Gitlin retains Gramsci's concept of hegemony as "a ruling class's...domination of subordinate classes and groups through the elaboration and penetration of ideology (ideas and assumptions) into their common sense and everyday practice" so as to achieve "the systematic...engineering of mass consent to the established order" (253). In our own society, this engineering of consent occurs in a process wherein "the culture industry as a whole" (254) presents "a hegemonic framework which bounds and narrows the range of actual and potential contending world views" (257) via "media products which ratify the established order of commodity production" (271): "Hegemony is an historical process in which one picture of the world is systematically preferred over others" (257). Thus, Gitlin's position may be summarized, in his own words, as follows:

I work from the assumption that the mass media are, to say the least, a significant social force in the forming and delimiting...of ideology.... they work through selections and omissions, through emphases and tones, through all their forms of treatment.... Such ideological force is central to the continuation of the established order.... the central command structures of this order are an oligopolized, privately controlled corporate economy...embedded within a capitalist world.... do citizens agree to identify themselves and to behave as consumers, devoting themselves to labor in a deteriorating environment in order to acquire private possessions and services as emblems of satisfaction?... *hegemony* is the name given to a ruling class's domination through ideology, through the shaping of popular consent (9).... One need not accept all of Gramsci's analytic baggage to see the penetrating importance of the notion of hegemony— uniting persuasion from above with consent from below—for comprehending the endurance of advanced capitalist society.... But I retain Gramsci's core conception: those who rule the dominant institutions secure their power...by impressing their definitions of the situation upon those they rule.... Hegemony is done by the dominant and collaborated in by the dominated.... Hegemonic ideology enters into everything people do and think is "natural".... it meshes with the "common sense" through which people make the world seem intelligible; it tries to *become* that common sense. (10)

A similar point concerning the hegemonic shaping of common sense and traceable to Gramsci appears in an essay by Said:

All ideas, philosophies, views and texts aspire to the consent of their consumers, and here Gramsci is more percipient than most in recognizing that there is a set of characteristics unique to civil society in which texts—embodying ideas, philosophies and so forth—acquire power through what Gramsci describes as diffusion, dissemination into and hegemony over the world of "common sense." (144)

Further examples of the position just described have appeared widely in critical studies of culture in general and of television in particular. Many writers have noted the manner in which TV bolsters the ideological foundations of the *Western Imperialistic Materialistic Paternalism*—what we might call the WIMP Culture or what Fiske refers to as "white patriarchal capitalism" (*Introduction* 126). Salient illustrations that deserve brief representation would include the following seven statements.

(1) Hegemony theory is the dominant approach of American Marxian critics of mass culture. In effect it synthesizes the aspects of media study by viewing mass culture as a fundamental ruling class instrument used to maintain political and social control through the production of ideological "false consciousness"...or "contradictory consciousness".... According to hegemony theory, the media industries are only one of several institutions that dominate class-specific perceptions of reality (Gottdiener 981).

(2) Hegemony...is a lived system of meanings and values—constitutive and constituting—which as they are experienced as practices appear as reciprocally confirming. It thus constitutes a sense of reality for most people in the society, a sense of the absolute because experienced reality beyond which it is very difficult for most members of the society to move, in most areas of their lives (Williams, *Marxism and Literature* 109-110; qtd. by Berger 49).

(3) The *ideological approach* views genre as an instrument of control. At the industrial level, genres assure the advertisers of an audience for their messages. At the textual level, genres...serve to reproduce the dominant ideology of the capitalist system. The genre positions the interpretive community in such a way as to naturalize the dominant ideologies expressed in the text. (Feur 119-120).

(4) Hegemony thus is..."that which goes without saying," or the givens or commonsense realities of the world, which, it turns out, serve...the dominance of the ruling class.... The media, as unwitting instruments of the hegemonial domination, ...shape people's very idea of themselves and the world; they shape people's "world views."... the ultimate determinant of thought and behavior is not recognized, because it is so all-pervasive and fundamental.... the concept of hegemony encompasses all that exists in a society (Berger 50).

(5) Hegemony describes the system of dominant beliefs...which holds us together as a culture...in ways which serve ultimately to maintain the existing power structure.... Television, which is owned and controlled by those in power, is the major institution today charged with maintaining hegemony.... it has the greatest responsibility for projecting a dominant version of reality and belief and eliciting loyalty to that world view.... It stands to reason then, that most of what appears on television will—for a variety of subtle reasons—tend to support the status quo. Television will focus on aspects of American life that most please its masters.... the rules that the media follow...grow out of basic democratic capitalist dogma.... We learn, for example, that "freedom," in its operational sense, is bound by the choices inherent in capitalist life. We are "free" to buy this or this.... We will be "happy" if we have certain things (Rapping 14-15).

(6) The mind industry's main business and concern is not to sell its product: it is to "sell" the existing order, to perpetuate the prevailing pattern of man's domination by man, no matter who runs the society, and by what means. Its main task is to expand and train our consciousness—in order to exploit it (Enzenberger 10; qtd. by Berger 47).

(7) Television's depiction of capitalism as an entire system...is relentlessly upbeat, clean, and materialistic.... Personal ambition and consumerism are the driving forces.... advertisements for a consumption-centered version of the good life...convey the idea that human aspirations...can be fulfilled in the realm of consumption. The relentless background hum of prime time is this packaged good life.... other motives and desires are lived out, for the most part, against the settings of a well-appointed good life.... This is television's fundamental politics...the values of a business civilization. Capitalism and the consumer society come out largely uncontested.... The presence of the medium is such that we don't so much reflect on the meanings or (most of the time) study them; we swim in them. Television inscribes images of the acceptable....

"Ideology"...means nothing more or less than a set of assumptions that becomes second nature.... Television can no more speak without ideology than we can speak without prose. We swim in its world even if we don't believe in it.... television adds up to American culture's impoverished version of itself.... the bulk of commercial television (along with most of the other media) reminds us to think of ourselves as consumers first and foremost (Gitlin, *Inside Prime Time* 268-269, 333-334).

Further, some writers have applied this view specifically to the case of our central focus—the game shows. Thus, Comstock et al. explain that "a neo-Marxist view would hold that television serves the economic system by helping to maintain the status quo and by fostering values which make viewers hungry, thirsty, and acquisitive consumers": "From this perspective the game show is a training session" (308). For example, Barnouw argues "that the very themes and substance of television entertainment derive from the needs of U.S. industry" and that "the game shows honoring lust for appliances...exemplify that hand at work" (*Tube of Plenty*, qtd. by Comstock 21).

Resistance

By contrast, a competing school of thought—first flourishing in Manchester but now spreading to the cultural critics residing on this side of the Atlantic—insists on the "open" aspects of the television text (Eco), the "writerly" (Barthes) or "producerly" (Fiske, *Television Culture*) nature of TV viewing, the "plurivocity" of meanings (Ricoeur), the proliferation of "aberrant decodings" (Berger), or the multiplicity of simultaneously competing subculturally relevant interpretations for virtually any cultural artifact (Gottdiener; Hebdige, *Subculture*; L. Lewis; Stockbridge) via a "negotiated" or even an "oppositional" reading strategy (Hall; see Fiske, *Introduction* 111-112).

Foremost in advocating this alternative position among those concerned with cultural studies of television and reminiscent of those who have proposed reader-response theory in literary criticism (Allen), John Fiske ("British," *Television Culture, Introduction*) insists on the importance of an active, negotiated reading of television programming. By analogy with the Barthesian "writerly" text, Fiske calls his version a "producerly" text:

In practice...viewing television is typically a process of negotiation between the text and its variously situated readers. The value of the theory lies in its...shift away from the text and towards the reader as the site of meaning (64).... Television is a producerly text that invites a producerly set of reading relations: the production of meaning is shared between text and viewer. (*Television Culture* 237)

Thus, Fiske insists on "the ability of readers to make sense of the text in ways that relate it directly to their social situation" (*Introduction* 157): "Different people read...popular culture in different ways" (160).

The essence of this view lies in an insistence on the power of *resistant* readings wherein various subsegments of society extract various congenial meanings from the same program content:

television [is] a text of contestation which contains forces of closure and of openness and which allows viewers to make meanings that are subculturally pertinent to them, but which are made in resistance to the forces of closure in the text, just as their subcultural identity is maintained in resistance to the ideological forces of homogenization.... a theory of pleasure that centers on the power to make meanings...is the thrust of what I have called television's "semiotic democracy," its opening up of its discursive practice to the viewer. Television is a "producerly" medium.... [It] requires the producerly work of the viewers.... The discursive power to make meanings...is a power that both program producers and producerly viewers have access to. (Fiske, *Television Culture* 239)

According to Fiske, the concept of hegemony must be balanced by an awareness of the resistance that always lurks just below the surface:

Hegemony theory argues that the ideological work...to win...consent...to patriarchal capitalism is not just an ideological practice but an ideological struggle, and that signs of the resistance it has to overcome can never be wiped out, that some always remain to fuel more resistance in the future. The consent of the subordinate to the dominant system is never fully won; always elements of grudgingness or resistance remain. (*Introduction* 185)

Increasingly, many critics regard this active model of the resistant television viewer as the new orthodoxy (Brown, "Conclusion" 210; Brown, "Introduction" 19; Gendron 19; Gottdiener 984; Marchetti 185; Modleski, "Introduction" xi; Morris 21; Press, *Women Watching* 19). Thus, for example, patriarchally macho men can view *I Love Lucy* as the adventures of a lovably daffy red-head whereas devout feminists can see her as the embodiment of a righteous attack on the male supremacy of her benighted husband Ricky (Mellencamp, "Situation Comedy"; Press, *Women Watching*). Indeed, in his sustained account, Fiske makes a strong case that, of its essence, "mass" popularity of the type associated with television requires not so much an appeal to the "lowest common denominator" of tastes shared by the hoi polloi as it does a polysemic flexibility of open interpretation that allows members of diverse subcultures each to extract congenial meanings resistant to the ideological hegemony of the ruling interests that would otherwise succeed in reducing them to the status of hopelessly subjugated "cultural dopes":

To be popular, the television text has to be read and enjoyed by a diversity of social groups, so its meanings must be capable of being inflected in a number of different ways. The television text is therefore...polysemic...a text that can be read differently by the discursive practices of different readers (66).... Television's...popularity among its diversity of audiences depends upon its ability to be easily and differently incorporated into a variety of subcultures: popularity, audience activity, and polysemy are mutually entailed and interdependent concepts (107).... In order for the text to be popular..., it must contain contradictions, gaps, and traces of counter-ideologies.... texts that are popular amongst a wide variety of audiences must hold this balance between the dominant ideology and its multiple oppositions (*Television Culture* 321).

In essence, then, Fiske views television and its reception as an inherently *pluralistic* activity in which "television is the plurality of its reading practices, the democracy of its pleasures": "It promotes and provokes a network of resistances to its own power whose attempt to homogenize and hegemonize breaks down on its instability and multiplicity of its meanings and pleasures" (*Television Culture* 324). Thus, when Fiske applies this approach to an analysis of reader responses to *The NewlyWed Game*, he finds "meanings that differed from the dominant and in some cases contradicted it" (*Introduction* 161). For example, "those sympathetic to feminism...were concerned more with how women coped with and struggled against patriarchal domination" and "found pro-feminine meanings that resisted and opposed the myth and its work in gender politics" (160).

Chapter 4
Daytime Television Game Shows
as a Regressive Case

When applied to the analysis of programs like *I Love Lucy* and *The Honeymooners*, *The Mary Tyler Moore Show* and *All in the Family*, *Dallas* and *Dynasty*, *Hill Street Blues* and *Cagney & Lacey*, or *L.A. Law* and *The Trials of Rosie O'Neill*—and innumerable cultural studies have done exactly that—the position advocated by Fiske ("British," *Television Culture, Introduction*) strikes me as quite convincing. (See, for example, Ang; Brown, "Introduction"; D. Clark; Deming; Press, "Class.") Clearly, these are (or were) shows ripe with alternative meanings for various subsegments of society and therefore "open" to a variety of different and potentially "resistant" cultural interpretations.

A viewer of *Hill Street* could identify with the disillusioned homebody (Faye), the blue-collar working woman (Lucy), or the aristocratic professional (Joyce). Similarly, the fictive world of *L.A. Law* has room to represent the interests of segments drawn from all walks of life (Jews, Catholics, WASPs, Blacks, Hispanics, straights, Gays, Lesbians, the mentally retarded, the married, the single, the divorced, the widowed, the young, the elderly, the innocent, the guilty, etc.). And *Rosie O'Neill*—that masterpiece of pluralistic charm—appears to have found a way to represent virtually *everyone*.

So, in general, Fiske's view of television as an "open," "producerly," "plurivocal," "polysemic" medium that encourages a variety of "negotiated" or "oppositional" reading strategies and inspires alternative "resistant" readings or "aberrant" decodings commands broad agreement.

24

Hegemony Redux

But let us also remember that Fiske has characterized the television text as "a state of tension between forces of *closure...*and forces of *openness*" (*Television Culture* 84): "This contestation takes the form of the struggle for meaning, in which the dominant classes attempt to 'naturalize' the meanings that serve their interests into the 'common sense' of the society as a whole, whereas subordinate classes resist this process in various ways, and to varying degrees, and try to make meanings that serve their interests" ("British" 255). Indeed, in the present study, I wish to emphasize the hegemonic side of this dynamic tension by arguing that *sometimes* a program or type of program appears that is so single-minded in its obeisance to the dominant ideology that its hegemonic support of the capitalist ethic and the ethos of consumption cannot reasonably be avoided by any plethora of potentially viable resistant readings of the type envisioned by Fiske.

Here, as implied by Modleski, the danger lies in neglecting to observe such clear-cut cases because of a failure to maintain "the proper critical distance" ("Introduction" xi). Making a similar point, while emphasizing that some texts are indeed "more open" and "hegemonically more 'leaky,'" Deming acknowledges that others are more "hermetically sealed" (53). Ultimately, even Brown ("Conclusion") must admit that "there are also situations [which]...seem so extreme that the dominant reading would seem to be the only one possible" (209). Tending toward this extreme, the situation with game shows appears to resemble that which Larrain finds for the case of Thatcherism in another context:

It seems...a return, with a vengeance, to the old and quintessential principles of bourgeois political ideology.... These principles can well be encapsulated in...the market, ...wealth and freedom of choice...opportunities to buy...and...the old ideological values of the capitalist system. (23)

The Claim

Specifically, I wish to claim that *occasionally* one does seem to encounter specimens of television text that appear "closed," "readerly," "univocal," or "monosemic"—that is, programs that invite only a "dominant" reading strategy and that encourage only one interpretation by virtue of proclaiming one insistent thematic meaning in their every nuance, their every facet, and their every detail. In this respect, such a "dominant" text recalls the tendency noted by Chambers for the Hollywood cinema to present "a closed representation of the world" that "removes the ground for alternative interpretations" because "all the filmic elements point towards a single way of understanding the events portrayed" (98). Thus, Press suggests that "in many respects television texts...bear the unmistakable marks of the hegemonic culture that creates them" (*Women Watching* 174): *sometimes* "television is...a reinforcer for the patriarchal and capitalist values that characterize the status quo" (177).

An example of this perspective, brought to bear on the field of popular entertainment, appears in Berger's claim that the latent function of football is "to divert people's attention from their real social situation...and, ultimately, to convince them of the justness of the political order" (113): "If football's manifest function is to entertain us, its latent function is to socialize us and offer us models to imitate and notions that will help us to fit into the contemporary bureaucratic corporate world" (112). Berger's analysis of news programs evokes an even more vivid impression of hegemony in the society of consumption:

The ideological assumptions...are not generally recognized...by the...audiences. That makes them all the more insidious.... we find an insidious commercialization present..., for they almost always contain, as an end result, the promotion of some product or service.... Ultimately, though these features may seem quite innocent, they serve as free advertisements for businesses.... From the sociological perspective, the manifest functions of these features are to entertain.... the latent function is to "sell".... they help support the ideological perspectives of the ruling classes and they fuel the engines of consumption. (130)

In this spirit, with respect to game shows, Fiske and Hartley once described *Let's Make a Deal* as "a syntagm of free enterprise, with the emphasis on the risk-taking, get-rich-quick version, rather than on the more sober old-fashioned one of hard work being the recipe for success" (151). Later, Fiske and Hartley describe game shows more generally as "a distinct television genre that meets a definable set of socio-cultural needs": "The core 'needs' that this genre sets out to satisfy are thus discernible as those which underlie a free-enterprise, competitive, though liberal, society in which winners are rewarded...by movement up through the class system" (156).

As Tetzlaff puts a similar point, "many contemporary popular texts...still articulate meaningful ideologies" (21):

Capitalism's needs in social control are...explicitly material—to make sure that people continue to work, to consume and to refrain from mounting any effective challenge to the system.... To the extent a cultural system can yield these results, and still provide motivations for production and consumption, it serves the maintenance of capitalist control.... The overall systemic function of popular culture within capitalism is to reconcile capital's subordinates to their position within the economy. It...provides enough rewards in the form of pleasure, escape or identification...to keep us coming back to the culture industry for more limited relief. (29-31)

In this view, some aspects of the capitalist culture combine to play a powerfully hegemonic role in our society. Such a cultural artifact or genre, I would contend, is the television game show in general. And such a program, I shall argue in particular, is *The Price Is Right*.

Chapter 5
Some Personal Biases

Before turning to an account of the game-show phenomenon as I see it, I must share a bit of personal background and some resulting biases that leave me unequipped to regard the game show as anything other than an insidious greed-dominated threat to all that is potentially beautiful (not to mention truthful) in Western civilization.

Stars of Jazz *Versus* Twenty-One

In 1957 and 1958, when I was about 14 years old, the best show on television was a weekly program from the West Coast hosted by Bobby Troup called *Stars of Jazz*. This program featured performances by some of the great jazz musicians of the day—Oscar Peterson's Trio (with Herb Ellis and Ray Brown), the Modern Jazz Quartet (John Lewis, Milt Jackson, Percy Heath, and Connie Kay in their prime), the magnificent alto saxophonist Art Pepper (seldom seen in public before or since), many of the prototypical Californian "Cool School" stylists of that era (Shorty Rogers, Bud Shank, Gerald Wiggins, Dave Pell, Don Fagerquist, Marty Paich, André Previn, Shelly Manne, Red Mitchell, Buddy DeFranco, Frank Rosolino, Bill Holman, Jimmy Giuffre, Jim Hall, Bob Brookmeyer), and some of the great jazz vocalists (Chris Connor, Irene Kral, June Christy, Nellie Lutcher, Jeri Southern, Carmen McRae, Peggy King, and Julie London). Judging from reissues and bootlegs that have subsequently appeared on obscure record labels, *Stars of Jazz* consistently offered a feast for the ears and (one imagines) the eyes as well. For a jazz lover, it must surely have been the greatest

TV show of all time.

But I missed it all.

I missed it all because *Stars of Jazz* aired opposite my father's favorite program—one that he rushed home every Monday night to watch with an enthusiasm approaching religious fervor in its intensity—one that he insisted on viewing no matter what masterful jazz genius was performing his or her heart out on the competing channel. I now know that the pattern of rulership demonstrated in our household on these occasions is a phenomenon that still prevails to the present day. Research has shown that—when push comes to shove, or zip comes to zap, in matters of disputed program selection— the Father is King (Morley 36). Today, Dad holds the remote control unit. In the late 1950s, the process was equally firm-handed. In particular, my father's tastes compelled the rest of the family, including me, to watch a quiz program called *Twenty-One*.

Sponsored by Geritol, co-created by Dan Enright and by its host Jack Barry, produced by Albert Freedman, and first aired in the Fall of 1956, *Twenty-One* featured one of the early quiz-show formats in which purportedly brilliant but nonetheless homey and lovable contestants got themselves locked into soundproof and (we are now told) unventilated isolation booths where they sweated profusely, mopped their brows feverishly, grimaced resolutely, labored mightily, and strived heroically to bring forth the answers to impossibly arcane and esoteric questions about boxing matches, baseball, food, love stories, movie stars, the opera, medieval paintings, Shakespeare, the Bible, or ancient history. (For general accounts, see Barnouw, *Tube of Plenty*; Boddy; Comstock; Conrad; Goodman; Skornia; and, especially, DeLong.)

Charles Van Doren

My father's favorite contestant on *Twenty-One* was a young English teacher from Columbia University named Charles Van Doren, whose showmanship in performing prodigious feats of memory simply could not be—and, to my sorrow, was not ever—missed. Van Doren emerged as a pop icon of the late 1950s: "He was billed...as a model of 'integrity and educational achievement' " (Goodman H31). Thus, his appearances on *Twenty-One* boosted the sales of Geritol by 40 percent, prompted 2,000 letters a week (including 500 marriage proposals), and won Van Doren not only $129,000 in prize money but also a featured spot on the cover of *Time* magazine as "the genre's most popular hero" (Boddy 106) and a position as the Summer host for NBC's *Today* show (Barnouw, *Tube of Plenty* 243). The quiz show itself maintained a position among the top five most popular programs on television—with *The $64,000 Question* solidly entrenched as number one (Barnouw, *Tube of Plenty* 187).

Loathing and Hatred

Since that time—for obvious reasons—I have, as a matter of principle, loathed quiz programs and hated game shows (a closely related genre). When *The $64,000 Question, Twenty-One*, and the others were finally definitively unmasked in the Fall of 1959 (though ominous rumblings had begun as early as 1957) as cynical hoaxes in which the favored contestants received the answers in advance, President Eisenhower compared the sorry episode to the "Black Sox" scandal of 1919, branding the quiz-show frauds as a "terrible thing to do to the American people" (qtd. by Barnouw, *Tube of Plenty* 247). In confessing his own duplicitous complicity,

Charles Van Doren...revealed that producer Albert Freedman had coached him in both answers and demeanor. Freedman told the college teacher that quiz programs were only mass entertainment and giving help to contestants was a common practice. Besides, it enhanced the acquisition of knowledge and the pursuit of teaching careers. Van Doren felt that he was promoting "the intellectual life" to the youth of the country. Later, he conceded that he had been "living in dread for almost three years." (DeLong 223)

I greeted the quiz-show scandals with a sardonic sense of satisfied self-righteousness. But it was too late. I had already missed most of the great episodes in the *Stars of Jazz* series, a deficit never to be remedied by repeats or compensated by reruns. On February 18, 1957—the night that Charles Van Doren first met Vivienne Nearing, the woman who eventually unseated him as *Twenty-One*'s champion (DeLong 214)—I missed the classic Jimmy Giuffre Trio (with Jim Hall and Bob Brookmeyer), the Red Mitchell Quartet, and Nellie Lutcher. On March 4—as Nearing tied Van Doren for the third straight time—I missed the nonpareil Oscar Peterson Trio featuring the guitarist Herb Ellis and the bassist Ray Brown. In my life as a television viewer, genuine culture (the magisterial jazz masters) had been displaced and corrupted by the lowest form of mindless trash (the phony quiz programs). And nothing could undo the damage.

Windows

It therefore takes some effort of will for me now to turn toward a clear-eyed examination of game shows in general, and *The Price Is Right* in particular, as potentially valuable windows on popular culture. As the direct descendants of the corrupt quiz programs, game shows bear a stigma that renders them suspect from the start as "the lowest form of television" (Fiske, "Women and Quiz Shows" 134). They reflect a sensibility derived from greed rather than generosity, guided by the selfish interests of big business rather than considerations of public welfare, and founded on shabby entertainment rather than serious enlightenment (Skornia).

Thus, for example, Skornia quotes the ad executive Fairfax Cone's characterization of the quiz-show audience as "the gum chewers, the lip movers, and the bulk of the no-opinion holders" (135) and reprints Walter Lippmann's scathing explanation of the quiz-program fraud:

The crux of the evil is that in seeking great mass audiences, the industry...decided from its experience that the taste of great masses is a low one, and that to succeed in the competition it must pander to this low taste. (247)

About the same time that Cone and Lippmann made their pronouncements in 1959, Dalton Trumbo added that the quiz-show scandal "reveals...a future rigged for the naked worship of things and self, animated by a materialism so primitive that it is...a future of true godlessness, of corruption absolute" (qtd. by Boddy 99). In short—from the perspective of virtually any reasonable ethical system or value orientation—game shows in general and quiz programs in particular descend from and embody all that is worst, lowest, and most despicable in America's version of the Consumer Culture.

Reasons For My Focus

Why, then, would I choose to focus on game shows and, especially, on *The Price Is Right*?

Neglect

First, it is almost universally acknowledged that quiz and game shows have received less than their fair share of attention. Thus, Fiske regards them as "one of the neglected...forms" (*Television Culture* 265) and suggests that "re-examination of quiz shows and their audiences has hardly begun" (280). Further comments on the neglect of game shows have appeared in the accounts of Comstock *et al.* (26), Boddy (2), and Rapping (10, 61). These lead to a conclusion voiced by Bill Lewis:

The ubiquitous game show, then, occupies a space in the mythologies of television which has failed to attract the kind of critical attention which it undoubtedly deserves. (45)

Popularity

Second, with specific reference to *The Price Is Right*, we cannot fail to be impressed—indeed, astonished—by the program's popularity. It ranks as the longest-running of all the television game shows in history (Schwartz *et al.* 585). It consistently rates as the most-watched daytime network game show (Landis). Meanwhile, its master of ceremonies perennially wins Emmy Awards for best daytime game-show host (K. Clark; King). Hence—if, as asserted by Schroeder, popular esthetics involves an analysis of what "sclls"—one could not ask for a better place to start.

Part 2

Context

Chapter 6
At the Epicenter of Daytime Television

Many readers—those, say, with jobs or other responsibilities that keep them away from the TV screen during the two or three hours before and after high noon—may have managed to avoid immersion in the televised stream of vacuity that descends upon the house at the midday moment when the homebound viewer might otherwise feel tempted to do something truly desperate such as listen to top-40 radio, visit the nearest shopping mall, or drive to the Burger King for lunch. Suffice it to say that—to fill that threatening void, that existential emptiness, that terrifying chasm between the morning talk shows (*CBS This Morning, Today, Good Morning America, Montel Williams, Donahue, Regis & Kathie Lee, Sally Jessy Raphael, Joan Rivers, Geraldo*) and the afternoon soap operas (*The Young and the Restless, The Bold and the Beautiful, As the World Turns, Guiding Light, Santa Barbara, Days of Our Lives, Another World, All My Children, One Life to Live, General Hospital*)—the titans of televisual titillation have found a formula for entertaining the masses while also serving the function of keeping the country going so as to sustain the future availability of that same audience in a self-perpetuating cycle. Specifically, the humble means to this lofty end is called The Daytime Game Show (not to be confused with the Primetime Game Show, which amounts to just about the same thing aired during the evening hours).

Types of Knowledge
As distant cousins of the old quiz programs that originally led to the aforementioned scandals, the modern descendants

share in common the fact that—in one way or another—virtually all of them place an emphasis on the public display of *some* kind of knowledge. However, the *types* of knowledge emphasized have evolved into quite a broad diversity of species and formats.

In this connection, Fiske (*Television Culture*) proposes a helpful classification of the different types of knowledge honored on various game shows today. Paraphrasing his breakdown, we might distinguish among those that feature (1) factual esoteric knowledge (e.g., *Jeopardy!*), (2) factual everyday knowledge (e.g., *Wheel of Fortune*), (3) human knowledge of people in general (e.g., *Family Feud*), and (4) human knowledge of specific individuals (e.g., *The Newlywed Game*). Here, I shall focus primarily on the contrast between factual and human knowledge (1 and 2 versus 3 and 4) and on the everyday variety of the former category (2 versus 1). [The classification of game shows into four categories— Trivia/Quiz, Word/Puzzle, Personality, and Kids/Teens—by Muntean and Silverman appears far less pertinent and will not concern us further here.]

Factual Versus Human Knowledge

To amplify briefly, the old discredited quiz programs (*The $64,000 Question*, *Twenty-One*) paid tribute to academic learning of an esoteric nature. (See, for example, the study by McQuail, Blumler, and Brown; summarized by Fiske, *Introduction* 151-153.) This tradition has been carried forward but watered down to the level of popular culture and thus made safe by some of the more recent programs that feature the ability to recall factual knowledge derived from historical events or from the trivia of "masscult" (*Name That Tune*, *Jeopardy!*), to decipher verbal codes based on well-known phrases (*Wheel of Fortune*), to perform feats of otherwise useless memory (*Classic Concentration*), or to concoct effective gaming strategies (*Let's Make a Deal*).

Indeed, the potential complexity of the latter challenge has recently won the so-called "Monty Hall Problem" a featured position on the front page of *The New York Times* (Tierney) due to a controversy over its correct answer that broke out among the nation's best-trained mathematicians and scientists (Chun, "Letters" 191). Similarly, the amazing feats of recall, hair-trigger reflexes, and sophisticated gamesmanship needed for success in playing *Jeopardy!* form the subject for a lengthy exercise in self-congratulation written by Trebek and Barsocchini and entitled *The JEOPARDY! Book*:

Contestants must instantly access their memory on subjects as diverse as Howdy Doody and Shakespeare, and do so with thousands of dollars at stake and millions of viewers judging every response. And these contestants must be able to summon facts while two competitors, equally gifted, are straining to do the same thing, only faster. (104)

One recalls that, in the film *Dying Young*, Julia Roberts is distinguished from her aristocratic lover by her familiarity with *Jeopardy!*'s trivia items as compared with his expertise on the program's historical facts. Thus, in popular culture, *Jeopardy*-related areas of competence can serve as shorthand for personal interests and educational background.

By contrast with the tendency of these last-mentioned game shows to emphasize the demonstration of some sorts of factually based cognitive skills, an even more common thrust dwells on the ability to display "human" knowledge by thinking like other people—in other words, to conform to prevailing norms—so as to give the same answers that have previously or simultaneously been supplied by common experience (*The $40,000 Chain Reaction*), by the studio-audience population at large (*Family Feud*), by a panel of celebrities (*The Match Game*), or by one's own spouse (*The Newlywed Game*). One might think that programs of the latter type would appeal to those with a deep need to conform or a profound desire to be just like everybody else and that winning would be synonymous with being as ordinary as possible (Fiske, *Television Culture* 278) in that "contestants are rewarded when they correctly guess what *other people* think" (Modleski, "Rhythms of Reception" 69). Nevertheless, stretching a bit, one can also imagine competing interpretations based on family solidarity, the shared glory of notoriety, the manifestation of empathy, or the wish for a disappearance of the self-other dichotomy.

In this sense, the programs that feature human knowledge might permit various sorts of resistant readings. For example, Fowles argues that "game shows rehearse the viewer's sense of how the world works" (49). Meanwhile, interpreting *Family Feud*, Fiske suggests that "the winner is the person (or family) who best understands...what other people are thinking":

The knowledge used in *Family Feud* has been developed to manage the family's emotional resources. It is knowledge of people, and how they are thinking and feeling that enables women to manage and smooth relationships within the family. ("Women and Quiz Shows" 138)

Factual Everyday Knowledge

However, when one arrives at the type of knowledge valorized by a game show like *The Price Is Right* (not to mention *Shop 'Til You Drop* and *Supermarket Sweep*), one recognizes that the learning at issue is of the most mundane variety—squarely within the category labeled "factual everyday knowledge" in the typology proposed by Fiske (*Television Culture*). Indeed, the everyday facts foregrounded on *The Price Is Right* (and the other shows just mentioned) entail information about shopping, about consumption, and about the Consumer Culture Writ Large:

A show that relies entirely on nonacademic and devalued knowledge is *The New Price Is Right*. Its skills are those associated with women, those of shopping and household management, skills which are often devalued or at least made invisible and confined to the private, domestic sphere. It is articulated not to education, but to consumerism. Of course it...trains women as enthusiastic consumers (Fiske, *Television Culture* 276).

In such cases, the pluralistic perspective pursued elsewhere by Fiske strikes me as less than plausible and even somewhat far-fetched.

MON(os)E(m)Y

Indeed, the shopping-oriented game shows seem rather clear, unambiguous, closed, univocal, and monosemic in their capitalist-serving ideological role as valorizations of money, as validations of the consumer culture, as paeans to possessions, and as a pervasive reassurance to the houseperson that household chores are worthwhile, that dutiful drudgery in the kitchen pays off, and that servile labor behind the vacuum cleaner leads to the promise of ultimate rewards in a Paradise of Consumption awaiting worshippers at the Shrine of Shopping, supplicants to the Monument of Mammon, and novitiates in the Celebration of Merchandise.

In this prevailing emphasis on "MON(os)E(m)Y," almost *everything*—every detail, every image, every nuance—in the shopping-oriented game shows moves in this direction, toward the worship of possessions and toward the sanctification of materialism. The knowledge prized is the knowledge of prices, of brand names, of product claims, of store layouts, of recipe ingredients, or of lipstick colors. The interpretations encouraged appear limited to those that value the household activities of the consumption-driven housespouse. If these quiz programs harbor multiple (much less resistant) meanings or permit pluralistic (much less oppositional) readings, this potential polysemy seems so elusive as to recede beyond the vanishing point or so ethereal as to evaporate into thin air.

Chapter 7
Daytime Television Game Shows and the Culture of Consumption

Make no mistake: The shopping-oriented game shows play a crucial role in bolstering the bulwark of The American Way. That is, they sustain the ability of the househusband in Bloomington, the housewife in Salt Lake City, or their oppressed compatriots all across this Great Land to endure one more noontime eternity of washing dishes, scrubbing floors, vacuuming carpets, setting tables, watching babies, feeding pets, folding clothes, pressing laundry, and generally fighting the good fight against the dread specters of spotted glassware, finicky felines, and ring-around-the-collar.

In other words—a fact seldom noted in the archives of consumer research—many consumption activities are onerous, odious, and even odoriferous. Few in their right minds could find the strength or resolve to engage in them without some sort of support system. ABC, CBS, NBC, and other national or cable-television networks provide such support systems in the form of shopping-oriented game shows that foster a deep and encouraging respect for the culture of consumption while making absolutely no intellectual or other demands whatsoever. They celebrate the act of consuming. They reward eager consumers. They prize the knowledge of consumption.

Going With the Flow

We might pause to marvel at the delicately balanced requirements that must be satisfied to fulfill this crucial function. First, at all costs, the program must "harmonize with the household flow" (Altman 44) and must avoid doing anything that would interfere with the viewer's simultaneous execution of the previously mentioned consumption-oriented obligations.

Distractions from the task of ironing could result in burnt fingers. Interruptions in the scrubbing stroke or perturbations in its smoothness of execution could lead to streaked linoleum or spotted tiles. Worse, any televised content that might cause viewers to stop and think would run the risk that—once stalled in the progress of their cooking or sewing, dusting or sweeping—they might never get started again.

As Muntean and Silverman repeat several times, "More than one hundred million TV viewers watch game shows weekly" (xiii; cf. xi, xii). Thus, cultural critics like Modleski ("Rhythms of Reception"), Altman, Mellencamp ("Prologue"), and Press (*Women Watching*) have emphasized the need for daytime television to mesh with the continuous but fragmented domestic drudgery of the housespouse in general and—despite the partial progress made by women entering the labor force in larger numbers (Goodbody)—the housewife in particular.

This view emphasizes the increased recognition of television scheduling as itself a form of discourse (Kozloff 45, 67, 70) tied to gender identity (Press, *Women Watching* 3) and premised on the assumption that "between 10 A.M. and 5 P.M....women will be the major viewers" (Rapping 134). Indeed, empirical research shows that women exceed men in frequency of watching TV during the game-show hours by a factor of over 400 percent (Comstock *et al.* 103).

Moreover, as noted insistently by any number of writers (Altman 42; Comstock 30; Comstock *et al.* 143-146, 294; Fiske, *Television Culture* 196; Fowles 86; Kaplan, "Feminist Criticism" 231; Morley 147-150; Press, *Women Watching* 17; Seiter 26; Stam 26), research also shows that the women in question tend to watch television in general (and therefore game shows in particular) *while doing their housework.*

During the morning (game show) hours, over 50 percent of television viewing is interrupted—that is, with the viewer not watching a set that is turned on (Altman 54). Hence,

the kitchen [is] where they expect to be watched, by wives spending the morning and the dreary afternoon at their indentured labour of scrubbing and scouring. (Conrad 8-9)

Modleski gives heavy weight to this haphazard, preoccupied, intermittent character of women's TV-viewing habits:

I would argue that the flow of daytime television reinforces the very principle of interruptability crucial to the proper functioning of women in the home.... her duties are split among a variety of domestic and familial tasks, and her television programs keep her from desiring a focused existence by involving her in the pleasures of a fragmented life.... the housewife's...entertainment must often be consumed on the job.... Quiz shows, too, are obviously aimed at the distracted viewer, who, if she misses one game because she is cleaning out the bathroom sink, can easily pick up on the next one ten minutes later.... Television...rhythms interact in complex ways with the rhythms of women's life and work in the home.... My point is that a distracted or distractable frame of mind is crucial to the housewife's efficient functioning...and at *this* level television and its so-called distractions...are intimately bound up with women's work. ("Rhythms of Reception" 71-74)

Indeed, though we have seen some movement toward dissolving this stereotype for many women who work outside the home (Comstock *et al.* 294; Goodbody), the reward too often takes the form that they now occupy two roles associated with two jobs, one in the workplace and the other as a household drone (Press, *Women Watching* 64).

The Validation of Domesticity

But second, besides fitting into the fragmented rhythms of the household chores, the game show must also meet the challenge of providing a rationale that somehow manages to justify the otherwise intolerable horrors of housework. The program must do something to make the consumer's drudgery of diurnal duties seem bearable or even desirable. It must serve as part of what Mellencamp calls the strategy of "containment" wherein women learn contentment with the "imaginary, blissful domesticity of a ranch style house, backyard barbecue, and a bath and a half" ("Situation Comedy" 81). Thus, even while insisting elsewhere on the importance of resistant readings, Fiske cannot help but acknowledge the hegemonic influence of the enticing ways in which commodities appear in the mass media:

Women's pleasures...and the commodities by which to achieve them are produced by the system of patriarchal capitalism that ensures the subordination of women; and in so far as women accept these commodified pleasures and experience them as real, they are participating in hegemony. By...accepting the common sense of the representations of herself and her future, she is helping...a system that only middle-class men can benefit from in the long run. (*Introduction* 183)

In short, to help preserve the status quo, daytime housewife-directed television must somehow validate daytime housewife-enacted consumption.

Some analyses have emphasized how this validation appears in the form of soap operas (Fiske, *Television Culture* 196; Modleski "Rhythms of Reception"). In line with our present focus, though less frequently analyzed, the game shows appear to perform a similar function. Thus, the game shows undoubtedly enact a self-justifying role by valorizing the lifestyle in which they themselves are so deeply enmeshed. Though several commentators have noted the tendency for this role of the game shows to be neglected within the area of cultural studies (Comstock *et al.*; Boddy; Fiske *Television Culture*, "Women and Quiz Shows"; B. Lewis; Rapping), it seems clear that the game shows do rise to the responsibility of validating the house-haunted aspects of modern motherhood and wifedom, albeit with varying degrees of success. They achieve this valorization through an emphasis on ritualistic repetition, community, and material rewards.

Ritualistic Repetition

Some such as *Name That Tune, Jeopardy!, Wheel of Fortune,* or *Classic Concentration* rely on rules, regularities, and other irresistible rituals to suggest the implicit argument that rigidly routinized repetition is somehow a good thing so that, by extension, one should cheerfully accept the obligation of rinsing that sink, shampooing that rug, feeding that collie, and cooking that spaghetti one more time...and then, tomorrow, another time after that. Thus, Modleski explicitly adopts Chodorow's view of women's work as "repetitive and routine" ("Rhythms of Reception" 67) and argues that "just as the housewife is required not only to endure monotonous, repetitive work...as a kind of bedmaking, dishwashing automaton...quiz shows present the spectator with the same game, played and replayed frenetically day after day" (72).

Community

This Sisyphean viewpoint is attractively amplified by those quiz formats that place an additional emphasis on commonality, conformity, and community—as when *Family Feud, The Match Game,* or *The Newlywed Game* reward contestants for their abilities to think as much as possible like someone else—thereby implying that if all other American housepeople copiously consume household chores, then the consumption of housechores must (like eating Quaker Oats) be the right thing to do.

Material Rewards

Transcending these appeals to ritualistically repititious duty and communal convention, however, some game shows also attain a heightened awareness of the most effective motivation for chorelike household consumption—namely, the only slightly disguised promise that obediently completing one's consuming obligations, acquiring knowledge of shopping skills, and learning the prices of all the products available for purchase lead to fabulous material rewards associated with the ecstasy of ownership. Specifically, programs like, *Wheel of Fortune, Concentration, Supermarket Sweep, Shop 'Til You Drop, Let's Make a Deal*, and—above all—*The Price Is Right* attest to the self-fulfilling premise that Good Consumers win Big Prizes.

Secular Theodicy

This secular theodicy based on ritual, community, and materialism—Justifying the Ways of Consumption to Man (and, especially, *Woman*)—suggests that those busy being Good Consumers at home in front of the TV while their spouses venture forth into the workaday world to win the bread, pay the mortgage, and meet the installments on that self-same 27-inch Sony have reason to hope for some Ultimate Reward in the form of a Big Prize for winning the Game of Life in which they daily play the role of Eager Contestants. As noted by Williamson in another context, "It is as if Western capitalism can hold up an image of freedom and fulfillment and say, 'look, our system offers this!' " (106). Perhaps, some evening, Spouse will return with a complete set of outdoor lawn furniture suitable for reclining on the patio (if only there were a patio) or a set of matching luggage appropriate for the next family vacation (if only there were a family vacation) or a speedboat perfect for spins on the lake (if only there were a lake).

This proliferation of tantalizing consumption-related images irresistibly recalls the description of "consumer capitalism" offered by Jameson ("Postmodernism" 116) in his account of "Postmodernism and Consumer Society" in which "the relationship between cultural production and social life" (123) leads toward a reciprocal influence wherein the postmodern fascination with "schlock or kitsch" (112) mirrors the value system of "postindustrial society, multinational capitalism, consumer society, media society and so forth"

(124). In this cultural rapprochement, "the transformation of reality into images" serves as "a way in which postmodernism replicates or reproduces—reinforces—the logic of consumer capitalism" (125).

Hyperreality

Jameson's focus on a reification of the "image" advances a step further in the work of Baudrillard. In *The System of Objects*, Baudrillard views "consumption as a characteristic mode of industrial civilization": "Consumption is an active mode of relations...on which our whole cultural system is founded" (21) involving "a *systematic act of the manipulation of signs*" (22). Hence, using italics, Baudrillard proclaims that "*in order to become object of consumption, the object must become a sign*" (22): "Everything is sign, pure sign" (23). What Baudrillard calls the "compulsion to consume" focuses on the "possession of object-signs of consumption" so that it attaches even to things for which one has no conceivable use (such as the aforementioned patio furniture, matching luggage, and speedboat) and thus "has no longer anything to do...with the satisfaction of needs" (25).

Indeed, according to a kind of Galbraithian logic that pervades Baudrillard's view of the "Consumer Society," "*the system of needs* is *the product of the system of production*" (*La Société de Consommation* 42). In this sense, like hysterical symptoms, objects become substitutable in their capacity to serve as the carriers of social meanings without being anchored in basic human needs (44-46):

Marketing, purchasing, sales, the acquisition of differentiated commodities and object/signs—all of these presently constitute our language, a code with which our entire society *communicates* and speaks of and to itself. (48)

In this way, the "ideology of consumption" socializes the masses to the point where "production and consumption are *one and the same grand logical process*" (50).

Thus, in *The Political Economy of the Sign*, Baudrillard follows Marx (and Galbraith) to claim that "production not only produces goods; it produces people to consume them, and the corresponding needs" (70). From here, it requires only a short leap of logic to conclude that the link between products (as signs) and reality (as human needs) has dissolved so that signifiers have been cut loose from that which they signify and the "play of signifiers comes to fruition and deludes the world" (84).

Hence, commenting on "Symbolic Exchange and Death," Baudrillard finds that the reality of signifier-signified (product-need) relations has given way to what he calls "hyperreality":

Today, the entire system is fluctuating in indeterminacy, all of reality absorbed by the hyperreality of the code and of simulation. (*L'Échange Symbolique et la Mort* 120)

With this hyperreality, there occurs a kind of "Seduction" based on a discourse in which the "circulation of signs on the surface" masks "the charms and tropes of appearances" (*De la Séduction* 149).

In such a hyperreal world of appearances, all things become "Simulacra and Simulations" wherein

It is...a question of substituting signs of the real for the real itself (*Simulations* 4).... all of Los Angeles and the America surrounding it are no longer real, but of the order of the hyperreal and of simulation (25).... Illusion is no longer possible, because the real is no longer possible. (38)

Thus, aided by television in general and by the proliferation of consumption symbols in particular, we find ourselves awash in a sea of meaningless, unrooted, dislocated, nonsignifying images: "We must think of the media as...a sort of genetic code which controls the mutation of the real into the hyperreal" (55).

Ultimately, in the view of Baudrillard, we reach an "Ecstasy of Communication" wherein television in general (and advertising in particular) "invades everything" (*The Ecstacy of Communication* 19) to give it an "omnipresent visibility" (19) until "the entire universe...unfolds unnecessarily on your home screen" (21). Baudrillard finds this "obscene" or "pornographic" because "it is forced, exaggerated, just like the close-up of sexual acts in a porno film" (21):

Obscenity begins when there is no more spectacle..., when every-thing becomes immediately transparent, visible, exposed in the raw and inexorable light of information and communication.... *We...are in the ecstasy of communication.* And this ecstasy is obscene.... it is the obscenity of that which no longer contains a secret and is entirely soluble in information and communication. (21-22)

At this point in his writings, Baudrillard begins to spin himself into his own oblivious ecstasy of communication and moves toward such seemingly undecipherable works as *America* and *Cool Memories*. But, before lapsing into his own ecstatic raptures, Baudrillard (*The Ecstacy of Communication*) leaves us with a rather powerful evocation of the sovereignty of *the image* in the culture of consumption:

obscenity and transparency progress ineluctably, because they no longer partake in that order of desire but in the order of the frenzy of the image. The solicitation of and voraciousness for images is increasing at an excessive rate. *Images have become our true sex object*, the object of our desire. (35)

Rule of the Image

This rule of the image as (sex) object for our desires as modern consumers appears to apply with special force to the prize-worshipping mentality that imbues the ethos of the game show. On any given day, one might watch Vana as she vapidly uncovers letter squares and vacuously points to the convertible that one might win if one's key matched its lock. Or one can empathize with the pretty but perplexed schoolteacher from Brooklyn trying to remember which square covers the other half of the bedroom set that she needs to furnish her new apartment. Or—best of all—one might engage in the ultimate orgy of consumption-oriented game-show fantasy fulfillment by tuning in on the hour-long event to which we now turn. This 60-minute program—*The Price Is Right*—presents an apotheosis of the urge to consume in a kind of gargantuan grandeur that becomes all the more riveting when one realizes what it undeniably is: An institutionalized Monument to Greed.

Part 3

The Price is

Right

Chapter 8
The Celebration of Merchandise

As its title so aptly suggests, *The Price Is Right* is *of* the Consumer, *by* the Consumer, and *for* the Consumer. Its skimpy but amazingly resilient premise for 35 years (since 1956, on three different networks, with a brief interruption from 1966 to 1971) has been that the efforts of contestants to guess the prices of miscellaneous products will endlessly fascinate an audience of like-minded consumers, especially if good guesses are rewarded by winning the products themselves as prizes:

"Come on down! You're the next contestant on 'The Price Is Right!' " was the call that propelled jubilant contestants down the aisles year-in, year-out. The audible trademark of *The Price Is Right*, it has reverberated over the air longer than any other quiz catchphrase—undeniable proof of the popularity of the longest-running network game of television. *The Price Is Right* bowed during the height of the big-money quizzes, survived the postscandals crackdown, gained in audience appeal, revamped its pricing games and expanded its broadcast time period. A generation later, it was as fresh and exciting as it had been when it first appeared in 1956. (DeLong 240)

[For details on the program's broadcast history, see Schwartz *et al.* 372-377.]

Celebration

As you slog and slouch your way through your daily circuit of consumption chores, the logic runs, how can you possibly resist a program that is so obviously about *you*? How can you restrain yourself from indulging in the consumption-oriented ecstasy of yearning for products that you do not have and the fantasy-consuming orgy of coveting possessions that you do not own? In short, how can you fail to participate vicariously in the liberating celebratory force of the national Enshrinement of Mammon in the televised Temple of Greed?

Merchandise

The role of "highly coveted merchandise" or "a truckload of household appliances and furnishings" has appeared in (first) radio and (later) television game shows since at least as early as 1945 (DeLong 103). However, close viewing of *The Price Is Right* makes it clear that the subject of this program *is* the appreciation of the consumer products that it gives away as prizes. In short, this game show reduces to one unambiguous, oft-repeated, highly ritualized formula: The Celebration of Merchandise.

Numerous writers have linked television at large (Morse 62; Stam 30) and game shows in general (Rapping) with a process of fantasy-based wish fulfillment:

If we understand popular culture as a form of wish fulfillment fantasy, we can better understand its appeal (5).... game shows...have an imaginative and emotional power that is bolstered by their apparent truthfulness and the supposedly realizable fantasies they engender. (10-11)

DeLong quotes Tom Buckley in the *New York Times* to the effect that "game shows continue to reflect the American dream of easy money and a free frost-free refrigerator in every home" (170). To this, DeLong adds the following summary:

Instant entertainment and prizes distinguish...quiz and game shows.... A show-business atmosphere apparently insures ecstatic winners, happy runners-up and even smiling losers. An audience of more than 70 million viewers from coast to coast identifies with middle-America people as they compete on TV game shows...[and] pursue the deeply ingrained dream to strike it rich, break the bank, hit the jackpot. (255)

Conrad applies this interpretation to *The Price Is Right* in particular, arguing that "on *The Price Is Right* acquisition is an effortlessly wishful association of ideas" so that "the more extravagant jackpots on *The Price Is Right*" are "otiose, ornamental, consumerist fantasy" (106). En route to the fulfillment of fantasy, like most other game shows, *The Price Is Right* preaches an unremitting ideology of consumption dedicated to an enthusiasm for merchandise, a valorization of materialistic success, a glorification of avaricious competition, and an elevation in the ethos of a consumer culture that extends to the reflexive self-vindication of television itself. This Celebration of Merchandise occurs at a level of intensity that sometimes reaches a nearly religious fervor associated with the Worship of Icons and the Gospel of Commodities (Jhally, "Advertising as Religion" 226).

Various commentators have offered the following capsule descriptions of this Consumption Ethos—this "enthusiasm for merchandise" (Comstock *et al.* 301), this "hegemony of success" (B. Lewis 43), this "strong appeal to...greed" (Hickey 63), this "competing avariciously for cash and commodities" (Rapping 62), this "production of the woman-viewer as a consumer" (Kaplan, "Feminist Criticism" 223), this "equation of material consumption with well-being" (Flitterman 95), this "ideology of consumerism" based on "goods we don't need but...can't do without" (Conrad 6):

(1) The game show, a form which places great emphasis on the dominant norms of a consumerist culture...demonstrate[s] vividly the larger ideological work of the mass media: persistently concealing pervasive social inequalities behind an unquestioning celebration of...material values (B. Lewis 44-45).

(2) A pervasive theme of television entertainment is the glory that ensues from consumption. Materialism and personal satisfaction through purchase...are prominent in the programming they accompany. The most obtrusive examples are the game shows in which the lust for appliances and adult playthings becomes the vehicle for crude comedy and envious identification. The emphasis varies from straightforward competition for prizes to mockery conspired in by eager contestants. The lesson...is that base motives are part of the human condition (Comstock 81).

(3) The most bizarre of these shows...base everything on knowledge of, and boundless lust for, current consumer goods...where guests must estimate the prices of various items.... they integrate entertainment, sales and information into a totally consumerist display of American life as exciting and fun.... the key feature of consumer ideology [is] the idea that consumer goods and services are in fact capable of fulfilling our deepest needs, filling us with near orgasmic excitement.... personal joy and happiness, emotional intimacy and well being are seen to derive from consumerism (Rapping 64-66).

(4) As I watch *The Newlywed Game* or...*Wheel of Fortune*..., I am being asked to assent not to anything in particular beyond television itself.... it suffices that we switch on to these and all other games, that I become part of the network, the circulation that game programs so excessively enact with their incessant permutation of people and prizes in a never-ending present of self-congratulatory demonstrations that television exists, that it works. Of course, game shows, along with the others, are in tune with the capitalist societies of their origin..., but they are primarily in tune with television (Heath 292).

(5) Ideological criticism is...pertinent to game shows.... Game shows, for example, offer structured arenas of competition, most often with the goal of winning lavish prizes. As such, they promote and extend the consumerist basis of the medium in varying degrees. A program such as *The Price Is Right* directly involves consumer knowledge as the basis of competition (White 151).

(6) American game shows...exploit the emotional yo-yo between the elation of winning and the despair of losing: cameras dwell in long close-up upon the faces of contestants and their emotions—one contestant who wanted a car in *The Price Is Right* was reduced to gibbering with greed (Fiske and Hartley 14).

(7) Game shows...are incitements to that romance of consumerism..., for they transform wealth from the product of our toil into a globally instant conjuration of our wishes.... the game shows are a training ground in the consumption which the ads idealise. The games played on *The Price Is Right* [reenact] an evolution from a capitalist ethic of industry and thrift to a consumer capitalism fuelled by greedy fantasy.... In the games, television celebrates the wealth which it both maximises and symbolises.... The game shows serve television's ideology of consumerism.... The customer

is redefined as the player.... the game shows proclaim the television set's function as a commodity, dedicated to the promotion of its fellow commodities (Conrad 88, 99, 102-103, 166).

Chapter 9
The Structure of Winning

Following Lévi-Strauss, Fiske views the typical game-show format as a movement "from similarity to difference" in which "this gradually revealed inequality produces the winner" (*Television Culture* 265). This progression achieves "an enactment of capitalist ideology" in which "such an ideology...grounds social or class differences in individual natural differences and thus naturalizes the class system" (266). Thus, Bill Lewis sees game shows as a ritualization of upward mobility via the Horatio Alger-like dream of rags-to-riches:

> The successful player gains the right to move from the desk to another playing space and with it the right to play for greater rewards. This sign of success reinforces complex and powerful myths of social and educational mobility. (42)

Structure

In accord with this ceremonial pattern of upward mobility, *The Price Is Right* pursues a carefully balanced, beautifully proportioned structure that unfolds as ineluctably as a Brucknerian symphony. The schema for this structure in the particular case of *The Price Is Right* appears in Figure 1.

As indicated in Figure 1, *The Price Is Right* follows a multi-tiered hierarchic structure shaped something like an inverted triangle. In this funnel-shaped progression, visitors from the home audience of television viewers come to the studio (following directions and responding to encouragement

Figure 1

Structure of *The Price is Right*

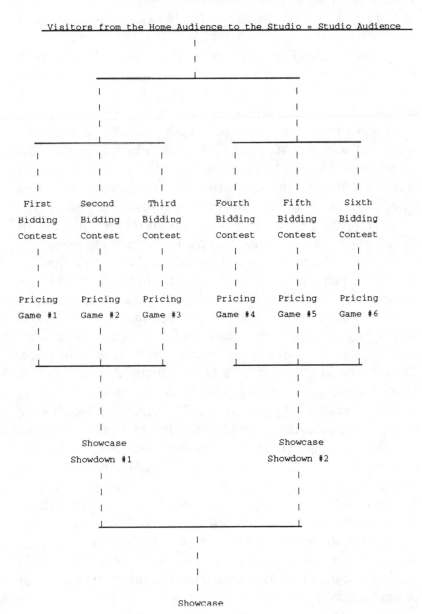

voiced during the show itself) where they may get selected as one of nine contestants who participate—four at a time—in a series of Bidding Contests. Those with winning bids receive a prize plus the chance to play a Pricing Game in which they may win another prize. After each Pricing Game, a new contestant is added to Contestants' Row (the bidding panel), and the Bidding Contest occurs again, followed by another Pricing Game. When three pricing games have been completed, the three players involved compete in a Showcase Showdown (with further possible cash prizes to be won), the winner of which earns the honor of participating in the final Showcase at the end of the program. After a second cycle of three Bidding Contests, three Pricing Games, and one Showcase Showdown, the final Showcase returns to the bidding format, with the winner taking home an array of merchandise almost too magnificent for the mind to manage.

If, from the viewpoint of social structure measured as number of participating contestants, the show is shaped like a funnel, from the viewpoint of prize magnitudes, it is shaped like an pyramid. As contestants proceed through the various stages just described, the number of participants decreases, but the prizes for which they compete rise steadily in price. Thus, in the 31 episodes for which I tabulated data (reported later), the average monetary value of the prizes in the Bidding Contests was $1,200 (s.d. = 385.2). Prizes for the Pricing Games escalated considerably in value and often included big-ticket items such as automobiles priced in the neighborhood of $10,000 or more. Ultimately, the Showcases at the end of the program carried an average price tag of $18,552 (s.d. = 6,713.9). Thus, the funnel-shaped pattern (9— 6— 2— 1) leading toward fewer and fewer contestants (from similarity to difference) is mirrored by a reverse pyramid-shaped structure ($1,200—$10,000—$18,552) leading toward more and more elevated prizes (the myth of upward mobility).

Prizes

In essence, then, the format is simple, straightforward, and structured on a foundation erected from the primordial building blocks of all game shows: prizes, Prizes, and more PRIZES. As one moves through the funnel, the prizes grow in monetary value until one ultimately approaches the Gates of Game-Show Elysium at the peak of the pyramid. Thus—a point that deserves maximum emphasis—the prizes, the merchandise on display, the gleaming products that fill the arena in which these bravely consuming contestants compete are the stars of the show. In this connection, Conrad views game shows as "a theatre for the cavorting of consumer durables" (121). Fiske makes the star quality of the prizes even more explicit:

the prizes are displayed in a fetishistic splendor, and made the objects of a ritualistic celebration (*Television Culture* 266).... There is a sense in which the prizes become the stars, and the visual climax of many a show is provided by the camera luxuriating amongst the glittering, brightly lit prizes. (271-272)

Chapter 10
The Studio Audience as Contestants and Participants

Stars, needless to say, deserve applause. And—responding to this code of recognition, this categorical imperative of television programming—*The Price Is Right* allows full scope for its audience members to express their enthusiasm. Thus, the "ecstatic excitement" (Fiske, *Television Culture* 271) and "frenzied applause" (272) encouraged by the prize-oriented emphasis of this game show produces "the extraordinary event of an entire studio audience applauding a rotary iron" (B. Lewis 43).

The Studio Audience
The program opens with the stirring promise, articulated by its announcer Rod Roddy (who took over from the original Johnny Olson a few years ago when Olson died): "Here it comes: Television's most exciting hour of fantastic prizes, the fabulous 60-minute *Price Is Right*." Meanwhile, a camera pans the studio audience; each member wears a name tag and claps energetically. Then, as if from on high, the disembodied voice of Rod Roddy intones, "Sue Johnson...Come on DOWN!"

Contestants
Commentators regard this process wherein "the characterized viewer crosses the line normally separating characterized 'audience' from 'show'" (Allen 95) to enjoy "the exposure on screen and the memories of a day in show biz" (DeLong 232) as the essence of game formats in general (Muntean and

Silverman; Trebek and Barsocchini) and *The Price Is Right* in particular:

This transformation of audience member into character is perhaps best exemplified by [the] invitation to "come on down" on *The Price Is Right*. We might speculate that a large measure of the pleasure we derive from game shows stems from the fact that the contestant is...plucked from among "us." (Allen 95-96)

Immediately, one audience member leaps to her feet—clapping her hands wildly, grinning ecstatically, jumping up and down, laughing uncontrollably, often covering her face with both palms, shrieking wildly, or flashing the Arsenio Hall hand signal via the circular motion of an upraised fist—and runs to the front of the studio, just beneath the stage, where she stands almost helpless with excitement while she awaits the announcement of the other starting contestants (looking very much like an enraptured cocker spaniel who, after being shut up in the house all day, thinks that its master has come home to take it out for a walk). Rapping describes these symptoms of "exhibitionism" and "emotional excess" (61) with an attitude caught somewhere between bemusement and revulsion: "Contestants...indulge in the most uninhibited displays of emotional excess.... these people will shriek, dance, cry, hug and kiss anyone on the set, and generally make what the polite world would call 'spectacles of themselves'" (64).

The Voice repeats its summons three more times, with comparably spectacular results, while The Chosen cling to their positions up front—bouncing around, giggling with glee, doing high fives, and hugging each other in the anticipatory bliss of a sort of demented love dance. A fair sense of the prevailing hysteria is conveyed by the following story of an excited contestant, recounted by DeLong:

The most imperishable incident involved a young woman in a very low-cut tank top. Olson called her name as the first contestant to come on down. She stood up and began to jump up and down wildly. In her joy, both of her breasts popped out and she ran undraped onto the stage. The audience went crazy. (241)

Participants

As these events transpire, the television screen is framed by a strange, yellow, oscillating, almost violent border that bubbles and sends sharp spikes toward the interior of the visual space—thereby helping to convey the prevailing sense of excitement. All this highlights the participatory role of the studio audience in the program—a dominant theme emphasized by various commentators (Allen 94; Fiske, *Television Culture* 272).

Throughout the festivities, the studio audience participates vociferously—applauding wildly at the appropriate moments (cued, one suspects, by electronic signals on the studio wall), yelling out advice to the contestants on stage (often with the result that the contestants themselves appear distracted or fall speechless with confusion), and constantly effusing the vicarious pleasure that comes from knowing that they too might be called upon to play the game and to take their rightful place up front at any moment (an illusion further enhanced and extended to the home audience by constant reminders of how home viewers can order tickets to attend tapings of the show). The latter effect is further reinforced by repeated assurances from the contestants that they are regular viewers (many claiming to have watched the show since they were small children), as demonstrated by their knowledge of the rules for various games without any need to have these rules explained. [On the preeminent importance of this form of preparation, see Muntean and Silverman 77-81.] Indeed, contestants who admit ignorance of the games, regulations, and rituals expose themselves to the danger of being ridiculed and treated as nonparticipating outcasts by the Master of Ceremonies (in every sense of those words), who at this very moment is poised to appear.

Chapter 11
Master of Ceremonies

Master

Then—emerging like a messianic figure from the back of the stage—comes forward a man sometimes known as "consumerism's high priest" (Wayda 96) who will serve as Master of Ceremonies or M.C.: BOB (No Pun Intended) BARKER.

The audience, cheering wildly, erupts into a standing ovation, which Bob Barker humbly acknowledges with one of his carefully crafted mini-monologues. These short introductory speeches from Bob Barker almost always include the following six components: (1) "Welcome"; (2) "Wonderful"; (3) "Appreciate"; (4) *"The Price Is Right"*; (5) "And now I want you to see the first item up for bids"; and (6) "Thank you" (repeated anywhere from five to eight times). Tapes of actual broadcasts netted the following typical examples:

I welcome you to *The Price Is Right*. Thank you; thank you; thank you. My, I thank you. I thank you for that wonderful welcome. And now I want you to see the first item up for bids on *The Price Is Right*.

Welcome to *The Price Is Right*. Thank you; thank you; thank you; thank you. O, that was a wonderful welcome. Thank you so much. I thank you; I thank you; I thank you; and I offer you the first item up for bids on *The Price Is Right*.

Welcome to *The Price Is Right*. I thank you. Thank you; thank you; thank you; thank you. That was a wonderful welcome, and I sincerely appreciate it. I want you to see the first item up for bids on *The Price Is Right*.

Thus, Bob Barker's opening words—so full of the magic of incantatory repetition—immediately establish the highly ritualized and formulaic nature of the program. Reminiscent

67

of Theodor Adorno's worst nightmare, they are manufactured and predigested; they are standardized and mass-produced from interchangeable parts (Gendron).

However, Gendron notes that "we must consider standardization not only as an expression of rigidity but also as a [potential] source of pleasure" (29). Indeed, as implied by the last name of its M.C. (Barker), *The Price Is Right* may resemble a carnival—or, even more, a gambling casino—with its proliferation of flashing lights, glitter-covered machines, shiny spinning wheels, sparkling game boards, and other indulgences in the paraphernalia of showmanship or "trappings of showbiz" that provide a "sense of the carnivalesque" (Fiske, *Television Culture* 277). And, as also implied by his last name (Barker), the Master of Ceremonies may resemble a salesman with a message to sell concerning the Unquestioned Desirability of the Consumer Ethos in which—no matter how much you already have—it always makes sense to Want More (whether or not you really need or can even use it). But this carnivalesque and casinoistic atmosphere of sales-oriented showmanship is controlled in the best tradition of patriarchal capitalism under the strict observation of a host of rules, restrictions, rituals, repetitions, rigidities, redundancies, and regularities. Thus, the overall effect resembles that attributed by Gendron—following Adorno—to the lower forms of popular music:

Perhaps nothing is as resistant to consumer reinterpretation as standardized forms, sounds, and verbal devices operating at the conventionalized core.... Because of their intimate association with constant repetition, plugging, and self-advertisement, these standardized components probably evoke the entrenched codes of the dominant culture.... The tendency...is to employ...devices, like standardization, that automatically call the dominant codes into play. (35)

This reliance on formulas, standardizations, and conventions as principles of efficient production in general (Fiske, *Television Culture* 110) and in game shows especially (Brunt

22) is well known. As one symptom of this formulaic principle of organization in the specific case of *The Price Is Right*,
one need only consider the music heard during the program.
To the extent that it is noticeable at all, it is entirely repetitive
and mechanical, as if designed for a tape loop by the rhythm
generator in one of those computerized keyboards that accompany themselves while the performer idly watches from the
sidelines.

Sometimes, amidst all this rigid regularity, Bob Barker
adds an impromptu departure to his mini-monologue in the
form of an improvised witticism such as "I hope you like me
that well at the end of the program," "I just hope you like me
that much at the end of the hour," or "I can tell from that welcome, you expected Bob Hope, didn't you?" On those
inspired occasions, his greeting goes something like this:

I welcome you to *The Price Is Right*. Thank you. O, what a wonderful
welcome. Thank you; thank you; thank you; thank you. I appreciate that. I
think those people over there expected somebody else. I want you to see
the first item up for bids on *The Price Is Right*.

Ceremony

As these examples should make amply clear, Bob Barker
is more a master of ceremony than of shining humor or
sparkling repartee. Indeed, his attempts to engage contestants
in banter are most often embarrassing at best, as when he
makes puns on the name of someone named "Tina Tamarow"
("I thought you said you'd call Tina 'tomorrow,' but you
called her today"). Quite frequently, then, Bob Barker disguis-
es the paucity of his wit by relying on various sorts of formulaic devices. I shall mention four of these as especially obvious examples.

First, Bob Barker repeatedly mentions certain historical
moments or commemorating landmarks on the show—such as
the first time that he himself entered via the right-hand aisle,
the first time four contestants bid within one dollar of each
other, the first time a man saved such a large amount in the

savings game, or the first time a woman pulled all five digits in the price of a car out of the pot without getting any strikes against her.

Second, Barker ritualistically reminds the viewer to "help control the pet population" by "hav[ing] your pet spayed or neutered" (a concept about which Bob Barker apparently has convictions deep enough to cause him to repeat this slogan every day at the program's conclusion). [In this connection, one must admit that Barker's love for four-footed creatures and his concern over animal rights are probably the most appealing aspects of his otherwise rather off-putting stage personality.]

Third, Barker continually makes essentially sexist remarks about the four good-looking models who parade around the stage and display the various prizes—showing off their flat tummies, shapely legs, bulging breasts, or other alluring body parts and mouthing such easily lip-read expressions as "It's delicious," "I use this," or "This is wonderful" while Bob Barker refers to them as "My Beauties" ("The Lovely Dian," "The Lovely Holly," "The Lovely Kathleen," and "The Lovely Janice," respectively). Thus, *The Price Is Right* retains a harem of slinky salesgirls" (Conrad 107) who "decorate the prizes" to provide "voyeuristic pleasure" (Fiske, *Television Culture* 226) so as "to display the prizes and thus associate commodities with sexuality" (Fiske, *Television Culture* 272). The result, of course, is that the models themselves are inevitably turned into commodities. One day, while modeling some water-skiing equipment, The Lovely Dian - who specializes in wearing very low-cut clothing and bending over voluptuously at the end of the program so as prominently to reveal her impressive cleavage while blowing kisses at the audience—accidentally held a bottle of Dove soap upside down, prompting Bob Barker to comment, "You know—even if she had kept that upside down, most men in the audience would never have noticed, not when she's standing there with that beautiful equipment."

[One must assume, incidentally, that Dian herself willingly participates in such affronts to her own dignity. Indeed, the December 1991 issue of *Playboy* features an eight-page spread showing The Lovely Dian herself in an eye-catching array of voluptuous naked poses (Wayda). The accompanying text praises Dian for her ability to meet "the challenge of relating to an appliance" and to "warm up to a refrigerator" when she "fingers a fridge's freon coil as if it were Mel Gibson's back pocket" (96). It would be hypocritical of me to pretend that I did not enjoy Dian's public unveiling. (I did.) But, given such complicity in her own treatment as a sex object, it would be hard to make a case for Dian Parkinson as a Champion of Feminism. Indeed, her pictorial in *Playboy* vividly recalls the aforementioned discovery by Baudrillard of obscenity in the "ecstasy of communication": "Obscenity begins precisely when...all becomes transparence and immediate visibility, when everything is exposed to the harsh and inexorable light of information and communication" (130).]

Fourth, Bob Barker consistently finds ways to make insulting remarks to the contestants. For example, if a contestant displays uncertainty concerning the rules of some bizarre, senseless, or inane pricing game, Bob Barker seizes the opportunity to ridicule that contestant for not having mastered the relevant set of instructions. The only way to avoid this humiliation, of course, is to watch the program religiously so as to memorize the dozens of pricing-game variations in advance, thereby presenting evidence of one's status as a True Believer. Bob Barker is impatient with the heathen who have not learned all the rules. He is even more contemptuous of those who do not pay him the respect he thinks he deserves. On one recent program, for example, he scolded a young woman who kept turning her head away from him to listen to the vociferous audience by telling her that she made him feel like Edgar Bergen (thereby managing to imply, of course, that like Charlie McCarthy, she is a dummy).

M.C. Versus Contestants

The capacity for Bob Barker to patronize, to insult, and ultimately to humiliate his guests (sometimes without their appearing to realize it) gains force from the program's staging and costumery. At the beginning of each round, Bob Barker towers above the contestants, who occupy a sort of pit at the foot of the stage in a kind of game-show purgatory known as "Contestants' Row" from which their primary purpose is "to escape" by making a winning bid.

Meanwhile, Bob Barker appears quite distinguished with his silver hair, his dark suit, and his nondescript tie—looking like, say, a lawyer, a mortician, or the president of a savings-and-loan bank. By contrast, the announcer Rod Roddy is a pudgy buffoon-like clown who dresses in outlandish costumes (reminiscent of a demented Doc Severinson) and who specializes in childish gestures, silly facial expressions, and grating vocal effects. And the contestants invariably wear exactly what vacationing tourists in Southern California would be expected to wear—namely, shorts, T-shirts, sweat suits, leisure clothing, and other undignified forms of attire. Visually, this places them (not to mention Rod Roddy) at a great disadvantage vis-à-vis Bob Barker in terms of clothing-implied status.

Generally, the camera takes only full-length and half-body shots of Bob Barker—never close-ups—while it often moves in tight for detailed views of the contestants' faces to emphasize the absurdities of the contortions that express their agitated emotional reactions. For most female contestants, one such emotional peak appears to occur later in the program when they finally get to climb upon the stage and to give Bob Barker a kiss.

I shall refrain from speculating about what quasi-nymphomaniacal impulses would make this experience so enjoyable, except to note that even otherwise respectable 60-year-old matrons are rendered somehow preposterous as they stand there in their too-tight blue jeans and Disneyland sweat shirts hopping up to plant a soggy buss on the cheek of this avuncu-lar-looking business-suited host who, within seconds, will begin to insult them to within an inch of their human dignity. In this connection, Kaplan ("Feminist Criticism" 226) cites the work of Aschur (a.k.a. Lopate), whose "discussion of game shows exposes the infantilized positioning of women vis à vis the 'inevitable male M.C.' " Conrad evokes this process of infantilization as follows:

Television's glory is the belittlement of people and the trivialisation of data, and the game shows are one of the medium's most playfully vicious institutions. Having abandoned the legitimate asking of questions, they not only parody their own original format but jovially denigrate their trusting contestants. (94)

Chapter 12
Merchandise on Display

At this point in the *The Price Is Right,* just after the initial appearance of Bob Barker and just prior to the first Bidding Contest, it becomes clear that all previous audience responses were only warm-ups for the entrance of the True Stars of the program in the form of the first featured Merchandise on Display. [On the role of display in the "calculus of objects," see Baudrillard, *La Société* 30-31.]

Merchandise

Perhaps the prize in the first Bidding Contest is an electric range with built-in microwave oven, a complete set of dining-room furniture, or a backyard hot tub and sauna. Whatever it is, it is introduced by Rod Roddy with enthusiastic language—amounting to nothing more nor less than a mini-commercial—as represented by the following examples, transcribed from actual broadcasts:

A new motorcycle. The Honda NS50F motorcycle—lightweight, stylish, and nimble—includes a lock-storage box, helmet lock, and aero front fenders.

A new grandfather clock. The Trenton clock was created with painstaking craftsmanship from solid oak—features a triple-arched bonnet, solid brass pendulum, and cable-wound triple-chime movement.

Lovely outdoor furniture. Mallin's ship and shore collection features nautical styling with royal blue all-weather covers; this rust-free group includes glass-top table, handy catch-all, and footstool—Mallin.

A new refrigerator/freezer. A G.E. 22-cubic foot side-by-side refrigerator/freezer—includes an automatic energy-saving system, adjustable tempered glass shelves, and convertible meat keeper.

Display

The fact that such descriptions amount to nothing more nor less than mini-commercials has earned *The Price Is Right* and other game shows their well-deserved reputation as "free advertising" based on "promotional puffs for merchandise given away on the show" (Conrad 101, 108) such that "the shows are themselves commercials" (Rapping 66) or "pretexts for commercials" (Conrad 99) or "the cheapest television commercial possible" (Fiske, *Television Culture* 271):

Programs themselves can serve as display cases for advertised goods. Quiz shows, for example, present catalogues of glittering prizes which establish a hierarchy of commodity values attached to brands and objects. (Nightingale 34)

Specifically, *"The Price Is Right*...becomes a sort of continuous advertisement as each new object and product within these games is described by brand name and qualities, often with a promotional tag line" (White 151). This promotional purpose is formally acknowledged at the end of the program when long lists of companies appear under such captions as "The following suppliers of products or services have paid for their use and promotion" and "The following suppliers of prizes have furnished them free or at less than retail." Meanwhile, Rod Roddy's evocation of the products in question prompts an effusion of emotions evidenced by screams, whistles, cheers, shouts, clapping, stomping, shrieks, and a general din of truly volcanic proportions.

Here, it seems, we encounter the essence of the modern Ethos of Consumption: the unrestrained, rafter-shaking adoration of Products on Parade; the unfettered, shameless worship of Commodities on Stage; the uncontained, mind-numbing celebration of Merchandise on Display.

Chapter 13
Agonistics

Bidding Contests

The excitement mounts as the series of games begins. First, in the Bidding Contest, the four players on Contestants' Row bid for the prize they have just seen. The one who comes closest to the true price without going over it wins the prize and proceeds to the Pricing Game, displaying the commensurate signs of joy en route. More than most writers, Conrad has managed to capture these aspects of "feigning hysteria on *The Price Is Right*" (96) in which "the jubilant frenzy of the housewives chosen to compete on *The Price Is Right*" (99) moves through "a compulsive hilarity" (101) toward a victory celebration of nearly manic proportions: "The women on *The Price Is Right* bounce, squeak and gibber like wind-up toys manically out of control" (102).

Pricing Games

In the Pricing Game, further prizes appear and the contestant participates in some sort of guessing game vaguely connected with the prices of big consumer durables or little consumer nondurables or tied to some other more or less explicitly consumption-related facet of the contestant's ability to "be smart" or to "get lucky." This is the only part of the program that permits any relief from the otherwise unalleviated repetitivity. Specifically, numerous variations of the pricing games do appear. But, on balance, these serve two redundant purposes that I judge to be common themes of the show as a whole.

More Display

First, the Pricing Game gives everybody still another chance to "ooh" and "aah" over the desirability of prizes generally bigger in value than those featured in the preceding Bidding Contests. For example, the prizes for the Pricing Games often take the shape of a new car or something of a comparably expensive nature:

A new car. A Buick Skylark 4-door sedan—distinctive looking, lots of room, comfortable, and generous in appointments— equipped with standard features and California emission plus floor mats. [Note that one cannot help but wonder if the latter item is an example of Rod Roddy's bizarre sense of humor or a typographical error in his script.]

A new projection TV. Pioneer's 50-inch projection TV with a smart remote control—includes built-in surround sound, a dynamic picture control, and an attractive rosewood cabinet.

A new sport boat. The Buffalo Mini Boat weighs 98 pounds; holds two people; three horse power; goes 16 miles per hour; includes horn, anchor, compass, radio, and trailer; from Buffalo Mini Boat.

Skill or Luck?

Second, the Pricing Game often manages to imply that the activity involved somehow bears on the contestant's ability to play the role of consumer in a skillful manner. For example, in the Check Game, the contestant writes a check for any amount; if the check plus the price of the prize equals from $5,000 to $6,000, the contestant wins the prize and the money in the amount of the check. In a game called "Lucky $even," the contestant gets seven dollars, guesses each of the four digits in the price of a car, surrenders one dollar for every number away from the correct digit, and wins the car if she still has as much as one dollar left at the end of the game. In "One Away," the contestant changes each of five digits by one digit in either direction; if the result matches the actual price of the car, she wins the prize. In "Hole In One," the contestant tries to rank six products in order of price (e.g., Caress soap, Centrum vitamins, Green Forest paper napkins, Pine Sol cleaner, Miracle-Gro plant food, and Ferrero Rocher candy); how far she gets from the lowest to the highest price without making a mistake determines her distance from a hole into which she tries to putt a golf ball (following the example of Bob Barker, who demonstrates this skill with devastating accuracy, going five for six in one stretch that I happened to view); if she sinks the putt, she wins the prize, often a car.

Other pricing games rely still more blatantly on sheer luck (such as pulling balls out of a pot until you get the digits in the price of a car or get three balls labeled "strike"). Needless to say, this intermittent emphasis on elements of chance fits admirably into the aforementioned carnivalesque atmosphere of the gambling casino (Conrad 168; Fiske, *Television Culture* 269; White 152). Indeed, for Fiske (*Television Culture*), this reliance on randomness "plays a vital role in the hegemonic structure" by providing "an ideologically acceptable explanation of success or failure" in which "the hegemonic function of luck is...to demonstrate that the rewards of the system are, in fact, available to all, regardless of talent, class, gender, race, and so on" so as to enact "the 'rags to riches' story which is such a potent myth in capitalist societies" (270).

Still other pricing games bear some semblance to what happens in actual shopping decisions—as when trying to save a minimum of one dollar while buying any four of the following items: Surf Detergent at $4.39, Cremora Lite at $2.43, Chuckles Candy at 69 cents, Franco-American Chicken Gravy at 39 cents, Superman Vitamins at $5.09 and Clear Eyes at $1.87. Often, such games combine the features of a shopping task with heavy elements of chance while providing another opportunity for Rod Roddy to run through a few more ill-disguised commercial messages—as when the contestant must try to pick two products that have the same price from an array of six items described as follows:

Klondike Ice Cream Bars—creamy ice cream with delicious coating, taste you can sink your teeth into from Klondike;

Capri Foam Bath with natural floral ingredients—luxurious foam—Capri gives you softer skin;

Carnation Instant Breakfast—when morning is a busy time at your house, stir up a glass full of nourishment—may be served hot or cold;

Oroweat Cornbread Dressing—a versatile ingredient for casseroles and a great stuffing for turkey, chicken, or pork chops;

Drake's Light & Fruity Cinnamon Raisin Coffee Cakes—they're 97 percent fat free with one third less calories and real fruit filling;

Surf Detergent is designed to remove your family's dirt and odors—Surf Detergent.

Showcase Showdowns

After winning or losing the prizes in the Pricing Game and after dutifully displaying symptoms of the appropriate emotions ranging from ecstatic bliss to abject despair, contestants proceed in groups of three to the Showcase Showdowns. The Showdown involves a Big Wheel with numbers from zero cents to one dollar in five-cent increments. Each of the three contestants spins this wheel one or two times, as desired. The contestant with the highest total under a dollar wins the privilege of appearing in the Showcase later in the program. Anyone who hits $1.00 on the head wins $1,000 and gets a bonus spin. If the bonus spin lands on one of three green numbers, the contestant wins an extra $5,000. If it hits one dollar exactly, she gets an extra $10,000 and automatically becomes so excited as to be a suitable candidate for the nearest psychiatric hospital.

Here, in running the Showcase Showdown, Bob Barker flourishes as a versatile if pedestrian stage-show personality. He devoutly explains every nuance of the Big Wheel's rotations, exhorts it to produce favorable movements, and exults in its lucky outcomes. Sometimes, he must help a little old lady or an elderly man who is too weak to spin the Big Wheel for the requisite full turn. One day, he killed about five minutes of extra time by pulling out his pocket handkerchief and attentively polishing the Big Wheel to an even more exalted state of brightness and luster. As one admires the gleams and sparkles of this giant instrument of fortune, one almost forgets that the whole business hangs on pure chance and that its urgent subtext can be encapsulated by a single word: Money.

Showcase

Thus, everything moves irresistibly toward the inevitable denouement in which the two remaining contestants face each other for the final Showcase and bid for an awe-inspiring array of stuff—say, an outdoor barbecue set plus a year's supply of ground round plus a chef's hat plus a Lincoln Continental or a dining-room table and chairs plus eight complete place settings plus an Oriental rug plus a Ford Mustang.

The episodes I have watched have included the following actual examples of combinations arrayed in the Showcase:

$$$ An entertainment center; a pinball machine; a grandfather clock; an old-fashioned kitchen range

$$$ A hammock; an exercise bike; a travel trailer

$$$ A home workout center (fitness machine, mini-gym, aerobic treadmill); a dune buggy

$$$ A pair of rocking horses; a big-screen TV; a superjet water bike; a new pickup truck

$$$ Trips to the Grand Canyon, New Orleans, and New York; a new Fleetwood motor home

$$$ Bedroom furniture; bed linens; baseball equipment; a trip to Toronto
$$$ A stereo system; a bar set; a Pontiac Grand Prix coupe

$$$ Red, white, and blue evening gowns; a backyard barbecue; a Maytag washer and drier; a California jet boat

In the Showcase, each of the two finalists bids for a different fully described set of stuff. Again, the closest bid that does not exceed the actual price wins all these fabulous treasures. The victorious contestant displays the full symptoms of someone experiencing an episode of ecstatic rapture. And the program concludes swiftly on this note of exalted exultation, often with the victor's friends, spouse, or other family members emerging to offer their elated congratulations.

Chapter 14
Flow: The Commercial Intertext and Audience for Brand Advertisements

Flow

One concept of considerable importance to those who apply the perspective of critical studies to the content of television programming concerns the phenomenon that Raymond Williams refers to as "flow." This concept represents the way in which televised segments—including the commercials—run together and coalesce in the experience of watching TV.
In the words of Williams:

In all developed broadcasting systems the characteristic organisation, and therefore the characteristic experience, is one of sequence or flow. This phenomenon, of planned flow, is then perhaps the defining characteristic of broadcasting.... in broadcasting...the real programme that is offered is a *sequence*.... the normal experience of broadcasting...is recognised in the ways we speak of 'watching television'.... On American television...the sponsored programmes incorporated the advertising from the outset, from the initial conception, as part of the whole package.... What is being offered is not, in older terms, a programme of discrete units with particular insertions, but a planned flow, in which the true series is not the published sequence of programme items but this sequence transformed by the inclusion of another kind of sequence, so that these sequences together compose the real flow, the real 'broadcasting.' (*Television* 86-90)

As this quotation makes clear and as numerous commentators have insistently pointed out, the commercials are very much part of the flow in the viewing experience (Allen 107; Altman 40; Boddy 9; Brunsdon, "*Crossroads*" 77; Feur 15; Fiske, "British" 269; Fiske, *Television Culture* 15; Heath and Skirrow 15; Modleski, "Rhythms of Reception" 67; Modleski,

82

"Introduction" xv; Morse 59; Rapping 170; White 143).

In particular, to cite one instance among many, Modleski (1983) focuses on how "shifts in television programming from one type of show to another and from part of a show to a commercial should be seen...as parts of a whole": "Here I would like to examine the flow of daytime television, particularly the way soap operas, quiz shows, and commercials interrelate. More specifically, I want to look at how the flow of these programs connects to the work of women in the home" (67).

The Commercial Intertext

Several writers have associated this concept of flow with the literary-critical notion of "intertextuality" (Allen 103; Fiske, *Television Culture* 15; McArthur 65; Polan 183; Stam 36) in the sense that "television produces texts that...point the viewer in the direction of other texts" (Allen 103): "Clearly...commercials...are *intertexts....* The deployment of a concept such as *intertextuality* over the terrain of television commercials...points to the fact that they...exist in relationship with each other, as phenomena shaped within shared cultural determinants" (McArthur 65).

One inference entailed by this perspective on the intertextual flow concerns the inherent difficulty of locating the television text (Caughie 51; Brunsdon, "Television" 62; Mellencamp, "Prologue" 6; Stam 35). Another highlights the important possibility of drawing conclusions from the content of the advertising that surrounds a particular genre—say, the commercials that accompany the daytime television game shows (Brunsdon, *"Crossroads"* 78).

In the latter connection, for example, Conrad suggests that "during the day the ads...concentrate on polishes, detergents, toilet tissue, the articles within the housewife's domain" (9). Modleski adds that "the project of many commercials" is "showing the immense rewards involved in being a housewife" ("Rhythms of Reception" 70). Flitterman agrees that "the products advertised" on daytime television include "a plethora of household items, defining and delimiting the role of good mother, wife and homemaker" (85):

The standard...advertising ranges from laundry detergents and other wash products, floor and furniture polishes, household cleansers, through diapers, children's toys, vitamins and medications, various food products (such as cake mixes, side dishes, cereals, snacks and pet foods), to a whole range of feminine products from cosmetics and shampoos to hygiene products, skin treatments and bath oils.... Daytime commercials affirm the centrality of the family and the important function of the woman as nurturing support system. Feminine needs and desires are often defined in terms of maternal imperatives.... Concentrating on the housewife's need to appear younger and more attractive than she might feel, many commercials on daytime television advertise diet plans..., various creams for younger-looking skin, and hair color to hide signs of aging. (86-87)

Audience

From the logic of this focus, it also follows that the target audience for the advertising on daytime soaps and game shows is assumed to consist largely of women in general (mostly housewives) and people over 50 years of age in particular (including a few elderly men in retirement).

Supporting this assumption, Comstock *et al.* report that "daytime viewing of...quiz and game shows is highest among women" and that "older women are much more likely to be interested in the daytime quiz and game programs" (115). Specifically, their data show peak ratings for daytime game shows among women over 50 years of age (113) with the audience profile during the late-morning game-show time segment broken down into 33.3 percent for women between 18 and 49, 25.3 percent for women over 50, 12.3 percent for men over 50, 9.8 percent for infants under 6, 9.0 percent for men between 18 and 49, 5.4 percent for teenagers, and 4.9 percent for children between 6 and 11 (111). In other words, women, infants, and senior citizens compose over 80 percent of the audience watching daytime game shows (with men in their working prime, teenagers, and children accounting for less than 20 percent).

More recent data from the PRIZM studies (Claritas) reported by Matelski and Thomas (21-22) suggest that game shows are especially popular with three groups of consumers, identified as follows:

T2 - "America's blue-collar, child rearing
  families" (18);

T3 - "Mixed gentry and blue-collar workers in
  rustic mill and factory towns" (19);

R2 - "Landowners and migrants in poor rural
  towns, agrarian villages and hamlets" (20).

One thing these three groups share in common is a relatively low level of education with the proportion of college graduates generally no higher than ten percent (Matelski and Thomas 18-20). Generally, they include members of families with children or people over the age of sixty-five. Hence, we may infer, daytime game shows are watched primarily by audiences from the lower socioeconomic echelons of society, composed mostly of young mothers at home with their children and older retired people.

Brand Advertisements

To tap these audience-targeted and flow-related aspects of the intertext associated with *The Price Is Right*, I kept an account of the advertisements included within the program during the 31 episodes that also supplied the numerical data reported later. A product-based classification of these commercials—aired during the show over a period of a month and a half—paints a revealing portrait of the program's consumption-oriented subtext and suggests the nature of the target audience toward which the full intertextual flow is aimed. Details follow.

Hair and Hygiene

As one would expect, the game-show commercials appear to be aimed largely at women with a concern for having

> *beautiful hair* (Agree Shampoo, Ogilvie, Suave, Sassoon, Finesse, Jhirmack Bounce Back, Salon Selections),
> *freedom from unwanted fuzz* (Nudit, Nair),
> *attractive eyes* (Cover Girl Eye Liner, Cover Girl Mascara),
> *odor-free underarms* (Lady Speed Stick, Ban, Degree, Secret, Arrid, Teen Spirit), and
> *proper feminine hygiene* (Always Ultra Plus, Summer's Eve, Vagisil, Masengill, GyneLotrimin, O.B. Tampons, Kotex, Sure & Natural Ultra-Thins).

These women presumably share with their husbands an interest in

> *nice underwear* (Hanes, Fruit of the Loom),
> *clean bodies* (Dial, Zest, Camay, Irish Spring, Coast, Lava), and
> *decay-free sweet-smelling white-toothed mouths* (Close-Up, Colgate, Crest, Caffree, Plax, Scope, Act For Kids, Certs, Freedent, Reach).

Clean Homes

Probably unlike their husbands, however, the target women are assumed to possess a deep fascination with obtaining

> the cleanest possible *laundry* (Cheer, Liquid Tide, Era Plus, Clorox 2, Stain Stick, Shout, Downy, Bounce),
> the shiniest or most spotless *dishes* (Joy, Jet-Dry, New Dawn, Cascade, Chinet Paper Plates),
> the nicest *woodwork and floors* (Pledge, Tarkett Lifetime Floors, Future Floor Shine, Carpet Fresh, Woolite Rug Cleaner, Love My Carpet, Resolve Carpet Cleaner),
> the tidiest *kitchens* (Hefty Steel-Sak Garbage Bags, Mr. Clean, Lysol, Arm & Hammer, Reynolds Sure-Seal Bags, Reynolds Wrap, Black Flag, Raid, Bounty Paper Towels, Comet, Soft Scrub), and
> the most immaculate *bathrooms* (Puffs Plus, Northern Bathroom

Tissues, 2000 Flushes, Vanish, Glade Plug Ins, Airwick Stick Ups, Renuzit, Liquid Plumr).

Food

Moreover, the targeted wives and mothers are totally devoted to feeding their families—especially

at *breakfast* (Kellogg's Rice Krispies, Special K, Raisin Bran, Crispix, All-Bran, rosted Mini-Wheats, Just Right, Nut & Honey Crunch, Fun Pak, Thomas' English Muffins, Kraft Touch of Butter Spread, Land O Lakes Spread With Sweet Cream, Fleishman's Margarine, Philadelphia Cream Cheese, Welch's Grape Spread, Pop-Tarts, Eggo Nutri-Grain Waffles, Nabisco Spoon Size Shredded Wheat, Triples Cereal, International Coffee, Taster's Choice, Folgers, Coffee-Mate) and

at *dinner* (Uncle Ben's Rice, Seven Seas Salad Dressing, Kraft Free Salad Dressing, Heinz, French's Mustard, Miracle Whip, La Choy Soy Sauce, Ortega Salsa, Velveeta Light, Kraft Singles, American Dairy Farms, Tyson Roasted Chicken, Louis Rich Turkey Breast, Kraft Eating Right Frozen Foods, Main Meals, Mrs. Paul's, Betty Crocker Hamburger Helper, Pam, Wesson Canola Oil, Hellmann's Mayonnaise, Prego Spaghetti Sauce, Raju Spaghetti Sauce, Chef Boyardee, Minute Microwave Noodles, Cool Whip, Jello Cheesecake, Jello Free).

Despite Mom's heroic efforts to feed her family, however, the kids are always hungry with

an insatiable desire for *snacks* (Mrs. Phipps Pretzel Chips, Planter's Cashews, Harvest Crisps, Extra Sugarfree Gum, Big Red Gum, Care-Free Sugarless Bubblegum, Doublemint Gum, PB Max Candy, Nestlë Bon Bons, M & M's, Keebler Elfkinds, Munch 'ems, Wheatables, Werther's Original Candy, Alpine Lace, Butterfinger Ice Cream Bars, Fla-Vor-Ice, Nabisco Wheat Thins, Honey Maid Graham Crackers, Teddy Grahams, Jello Pudding Pops, Crunch 'n' Munch, Baskin Robbins, TCBY) and

an unquenchable *thirst* (Classic Coke, Minute Maid Orange Soda, Welch's Grape Juice, Country Time Lemonade, 4C Iced Tea, Diet Squirt, Dole Juice, Sunny Delight Juice, Libby Juicy Juice, Crystal Light Fruit Drink, A&W Root Beer).

Nurturance

Meanwhile, the kids keep playing in the poison ivy and scratching themselves in the bushes so that they need a panoply of itching remedies, rash medicines, healing formulas, and other *first-aid items* (Cortaid, Caladryl Clear, Lanacane, Cortizone-5, Neosporin, Dermarest, Benadryl, Band Aid).

Among the younger women, some prospective new mothers keep a close eye on their diagnostic *Pregnancy tests* (Fact Plus, First Response, EPT) and stock up on *products for the new baby* (Huggies, Pampers, Baby Fresh, Gerber Baby Formula, Carnation Follow-Up Formula, Evenflo Disposable bottles, Johnson's Baby Oil, Water Babies).

Those not lucky enough to have babies focus on *treats for their pets* (Mighty Dog, Purina One, Meaty Bone, Pedigree Dog Food, Reward Dog Food, Friskies Cat Food, Control Cat Litter).

Aging

Women starting to age have begun to worry about maintaining

> soft wrinkle-free *skin* (Vaseline Intensive Care Sunscreen, Shade Sunblock, Oil of Olay, Ponds Cold Creme, Noxema, Clear Away Wart Remover, Dr. Scholl's Corn Remover),
> *weight control* (Dexatrim, Acutrim, Ultra Slim-Fast, NutraSweet, Equal),
> *graying hair* (Loving Care, Clairol Ultress),
> *hemorrhoids* (Tucks Pads), and
> adequate iron-rich *vitamins* (Centrum, Geritol Extend).

As they approach the status of senior citizens, these women are joined in front of the television by their retired husbands so that, together, the elderly couples devote their attention to

> relieving *aches and pains* (Aspercreme, Anacin Arthritis Pain Formula, Advil, Motrin, Tylenol, Ben-Gay, Exedrin, Ecotrin,

Midol, Anbesol, Doan's),

maintaining *regularity* (Metamucil Fiber Wafers, Fleet Suppositories, Ex-Lax, Fiber Con Laxative, Doxidan, Sunsweet Prune Juice, Sunsweet Pitted Prunes),

fighting *gas pain, indigestion,* or *diarrhea* (Mylicon Gas, Gas-X, Riopan Plus 2, Rolaids, Alka-Selzer, Kaopectate),

getting to *sleep* (Unisom, Nytol, Sominex, Sleepinal),

avoiding *salt* (Mrs. Dash, Papa Dash),

coping with *dentures* (Polident, Efferdent, Fixodent, ORAfix, Sea-Band),

overcoming *hearing loss* (Miracle Ear), or

combating *incontinence* (Depend Undergarments, Attends Undergarments).

Inferred Target Audiences

All this suggests a fairly consistent picture of the demographics, lifestyles, and customer values attributable to the audience segments who watch the game shows in general and *The Price Is Right* in particular. The target audiences appear to consist primarily of housewives perplexed by their daily chores; mothers with an obsession for feeding their families, bathing their babies, or pampering their pets; and senior citizens of both sexes as they confront the indignities of old age that only a heavy dose of materialistic consumption in the commercial culture can hope to cure.

Part 4

Testing A

Competing

Interpretation

Chapter 15
The Competing Interpretation:
A Resistant Reading and a Key Premise

By now, the reader might well wonder—in the face of so many textual, subtextual, and intertextual elements all pointing in the same direction and converging on a rather closed, readerly, univocal, monosemic, dominant reading of *The Price Is Right* as what I have called a Celebration of Merchandise—how one could possibly construct and maintain the kind of resistant (negotiated or oppositional) interpretation espoused as the foundation of the perspective brought to cultural studies by authors such as Fiske ("British;" *Television Culture*; *Introduction*). I have already implied that my own answer to this question leans strongly in the direction of a conviction that one *cannot*. However, I must also report that Fiske (*Television Culture*, "Women and Quiz Shows") *does* try to find a resistant reading for *The Price Is Right*.

A Resistant Reading

Given that I disagree with the competing interpretation of *The Price Is Right* offered by Fiske (*Televison Culture*; "Women and Quiz Shows"), it might be most fair to quote it at some length in his own words:

The New Price Is Right...contains also the elements of a countertext, one "written" by the consumers. In this show these skills are first of all made public and the person who uses them best is given a public acclaim that at times verges on the riotous.... Translating the womanly skills and knowledge out of the private sphere into the public gives them a status normally reserved for the masculine.... The ecstatic public acclaim given by the studio audience to the winner is...contrasted with the taken-for-grantedness of such skills in their normal family setting. (Fiske, *Television*

93

Culture 276)

Fiske admits that "quiz shows are a cultural product of consumer capitalism":

They foreground commodities, they blur the distinctions between themselves and the commercials embedded in them and the rewards that they offer are those of the commodity system. In short, they relentlessly address and position the woman as housewife and consumer. ("Women and Quiz Shows" 135)

But he is intent on saving an interpretation that maintains the possibility of a resistant reading: "I would argue that women can use commodities (and quiz shows as cultural commodities) in ways that negate or evade the economic and gender power of the system that produces and distributes them" (135). Toward this end, he constructs a view of *The Price Is Right* as a demonstration of feminine competence:

The New Price is Right is the consumerist quiz show par excellence (135).... the knowledge required is what our society treats as 'women's' knowledge: that of the prices and comparative values of commodities (135-136).... *The New Price is Right* is characterized by noise, cheering and applause.... the successes of the consumer contestants are wildly applauded.... the game-show audience's enthusiasm...give[s] public noisy acclaim to skills that are ordinarily silenced (136).... In *The New Price is Right*, money is replaced by knowledge: masculine money by feminine knowledge.... *The New Price is Right* treats the skills of consumption in a way that removes them from the sphere of subjugated, silenced domestic labour and repositions them in the sphere of liberated, acclaimed public leisure and fun. (Fiske, "Women and Quiz Shows" 137)

Later, Fiske ("Women and Quiz Shows") repeats this point as his main conclusion:

quiz shows are popular with women...because they bear not only the ideological voices of the dominant, but also the opportunity to resist, evade or negotiate with these voices (142).... *The New Price is Right* expresses...consumption...as a means of women's creativity and power.... The popular appeal of quiz shows for women lies in...the act of making the discourses of subordination into ones of empowerment. (143)

A Key Premise

Notice that this resistant reading depends heavily on the key premise that contestants on *The Price Is Right* really do display some sort of consumption-related expertise, shopping skills, or knowledge of product prices. After proposing the interpretation quoted earlier, Fiske immediately makes this important assumption explicit:

> The carnivalesque pleasures of *The New Price Is Right*...derive from a reversal of the normal power relations between consumers and producers. The consumer is momentarily liberated from economic subjection: her knowledge of prices and value...allows shopping skills to become agents of empowerment. They become the means of beating the economic system. (*Television Culture* 277)

To this, Fiske adds: "The winner is the one who best judges commodity prices and values; who is, in other words, the best shopper" ("Women and Quiz Shows" 136).

A summary by Brown ("Introduction") supports this reading of Fiske (*Television Culture*, "Women and Quiz Shows"). According to Brown, "John Fiske contends that...Women's skills at shopping, bargain hunting and understanding people form the basis of many games": "*The Price is Right*...recognizes women's skills as shoppers" (21).

This key premise that "in shows like *The New Price Is Right*...the winner is the one who best knows the values of a wide range of commodities" (Fiske, *Televison Culture* 267) not only underpins the resistant reading offered by Fiske but also commands allegiance from a number of other interpreters. For example, Fabe points out that "by rewarding shrewd bidding on small grocery items as well as on lavish showcases, ...it made a virtue of being a thrifty, knowledgeable shopper": "Everyone in the audience became a vociferous consumer expert" (181; cited by DeLong 240). Conrad suggests that "the games played on *The Price Is Right* test the housewife's memory of what groceries cost" (99): "The women on *The Price Is Right*...can win only if they've taught themselves to memorise supermarket prices" (107). Similarly, White explicitly assumes that "a program such as *The Price Is Right* directly involves consumer knowledge as the basis of competition, with success or failure based on contestants' ability to estimate the retail value of a wide range of products including furniture, cars, vacations, jewelry, groceries, and household appliances": "participants are subjected to a variety of games that require them to demonstrate their skill as a consumer" (151). Meanwhile, Nightingale comments that "contestants...compete in...putting their shopping skills to the test" (34).

While repeatedly watching *The Price Is Right*, I became increasingly curious about the validity of the crucial assumption made by Fiske, Conrad, White, and many others that this game show's contestants really do possess some kind of special consumer expertise, some impressive sorts of shopping skills, or some real knowledge about product prices. As we have seen, Fiske relies on this key premise to bolster his claim concerning the possibility of a resistant reading for this particular game show. The assumption therefore deserves to be tested against the empirical evidence of viewing experience.

Chapter 16
The Empirical Evidence

To address this empirical question, I taped 31 episodes of *The Price Is Right* shown during the six-week period between May 22 and July 4, 1991. Using data provided by these shows, I performed some statistical analyses on the bidding behavior displayed in the Bidding Contests and in the concluding Showcase. To preview briefly, the results of these analyses question the assumption made by some commentators. Their key premise concerning the contestants' possession of special consumer expertise, finely tuned shopping skills, or highly developed knowledge of product prices represents at best a serious exaggeration and more likely a badly distorted misimpression with no foundation in fact.

Guessing

When carefully watching the behavior of participants engaged in the Bidding Contest, one can scarcely avoid a recognition that they adopt the mentality of befuddled players involved in a rather frivolous and capricious guessing game. Indeed, the empirical evidence concerning their performance tends to support this impression. Thus, over 186 observations (based on six repetitions in each of 31 programs), the average correlation (root mean r-squared) between the actual prices of the merchandise in question and the first, second, third, and fourth bids is only $r = 0.37$—implying a typical proportion of explained variance in actual price of only about 14 percent.

If one combines the four bids into an average four-item bidding index, one obtains slightly better results—with an overall correlation of r = 0.47 (N = 186, p < 0.0001), suggesting an explained variance of about 22 percent. But the internal consistency of this average bidding index (as measured by coefficient alpha) is quite disappointing: a = 0.48. This latter result indicates that, as a measure of consensus among the four contestants, the average four-item bidding index has rather poor reliability.

Adjustments

Some consolation among cultural critics looking for demonstrated knowledge of product prices might stem from the fact that the accuracy of the bids improves from the first to the third before declining somewhat on the fourth bid: r = 0.18, 0.35, 0.49, and 0.41, respectively. This trend implies that some sort of learning process might occur as the bids unfold. Indeed, close scrutiny of the contestants' bidding behavior suggests that two phenomena require attention in this respect.

First, as reflected by the low correlation for the first bid (r = 0.18), this bid comes from the newest member of the four-person panel in Contestants' Row. These new players are often so nervous that they make silly mistakes such as forgetting where to put the decimal point. Thus, for example, they often say "thousand" when they mean to say "hundred," thereby overbidding by grostesque amounts. It therefore makes sense to deflate bids greater than $4,000 by a factor of ten so as to represent the true intentions of the contestants. [Note that, needless to say, mistakes of the type just described give Bob Barker endless material for the subsequent humiliation of the hapless contestants involved.]

Second, as reflected by the drop in correlation from the third to the fourth bid (r = 0.49 to 0.41), the contestant who bids last sometimes feels that all the other bids are too high and therefore bids $1 or $5 to cover all the ground beneath the previous lowest bid. The only information that this rock-bottom bid really conveys is the contestant's belief that the actual price is at least one dollar less than the previous lowest bid. It therefore makes sense to adjust bids of less than $100 to equal the previous lowest bid minus one dollar.

The two adjustments just described bring the predictive accuracy of the four bids into greater parity: r = 0.46, 0.47, 0.50, and 0.54, respectively. Here, the average correlation (root mean r-squared) is r = 0.49—implying an explained variance in actual price of about 24 percent.

Further, internal consistency for the four adjusted bids (measured by coefficient alpha) climbs to a higher level: a = 0.85. And the predictive performance of the average four-item bidding index rises to r = 0.59 (N = 186, p < 0.0001)— implying an explained variance in actual prices of about 35 percent.

So the information about prices embedded in the contestants' adjusted bids implies an explained variance in prices of about 24 percent for the single bids and of about 35 percent for the pooled four-item average bids. Both figures are considerably better than those of 14 (versus 24) and 22 (versus 35) implied by the raw bids before adjustments for nervousness and gaming strategies. Nevertheless, both fall far short of the level of explained variance that we could reasonably regard as showing real skill or expertise. By even the most charitable interpretation, the pooled wisdom of the four participants in the Bidding Contest leaves two-thirds of the variance in prices unexplained.

Endgame

One further window on the performance of contestants as price estimators looks at the accuracy of their bids in the final Showcase. Here, an impressionistic critic might suppose that—by virtue of the funnel-shaped weeding-out process described earlier—the program's ritual of gamesmanship would have selected the expert consumers, smart shoppers, or pricing mavens from among the other contestants who would have tended to fall by the wayside. One might therefore expect the bidding performance of the two remaining players to rise noticeably above the levels established earlier for those in Contestants' Row.

However, anyone who expected that would tend to be badly disappointed.

The 31 episodes on which data were collected yielded 62 pairs of bids and actual prices on which to test the expectation in question. These bids are single-item scales rather than four-item averages and should therefore be compared with the average (root mean-squared) single-item correlations reported earlier. Here, the correlation of interest in the Showcase is $r = 0.50$ ($N = 62$, $p < 0.0001$). This compares quite closely with the average correlation of $r = 0.49$ achieved by the adjusted bids of the individual participants in the Bidding Contests.

In other words, explained variance in actual prices remains at about twenty-five percent, even for those contestants whose perceived consumer expertise, shopping skills, and knowledge of product prices appear to have been validated by the elaborate screening process from which they have emerged successfully. Or, to put the same point somewhat differently, the champions of *The Price Is Right* tend to leave about three-quarters of the variation in prices unexplained.

Misinterpretation

One might conceivably make a last-ditch attempt to "save" a resistant reading for *The Price Is Right* by purposely misinterpreting the statistical evidence in light of an obvious statistical artifact contained within the data. Specifically, if somewhat perversely, one could focus on the correlation between the price of the merchandise in the Bidding Contest and the level of the *winning* bid (that is, the one that—in retrospect—came closest without exceeding the actual price of the merchandise). Over 186 observations, this correlation between winning bids and actual prices was $r = 0.83$ ($p < 0.0001$). If willfully misinterpreted, this statistical artifact (which relies on selecting the most "accurate" bid after the fact) would fallaciously suggest that the most "expert" contestants account for over two-thirds (about 69 percent) of the variance in actual prices.

However, such a misreading of the empirical evidence would violate the most basic rationale espoused by those dedicated to arguing for resistant interpretations. Such cultural critics wish to show that members of the audience are *not* "cultural dopes." Thus, writers like Hall and Fiske wish to argue *against* the notion that mass audiences are "duped" by the media (Larrain 7, 17). For example, Fiske considers "the meanings that quiz shows might have for their women fans," attempts "to account...for their popularity with women by means other than the 'cultural dope' theory," and concludes that "women are not cultural dopes" ("Women and Quiz Shows" 140).

To assume that people cannot recognize a guessing game when they see one but are instead misled by an obvious perversion of statistics would assume that they are dumber than "dopes" and worse than "duped." It would assume that they are downright stupid.

Summary

In sum, when tested empirically, the level of performance achieved by even the best players on *The Price Is Right* corresponds to an informative proportional reduction in error of only about one-quarter. Hence, three-quarters of the true price information remains as error variance.

When all is said and done, these contestants demonstrate a knowledge, say, that a car costs more than a couch or that a trip to Hong Kong costs more than a weekend in Las Vegas (if you start from Hollywood). But they do not demonstrate much more than that.

In this sense, the misimpression of pricing knowledge suggested by *The Price Is Right* to cultural critics in search of resistant readings is as big a scam as the rigged implication during the 1950s that Charles Van Doren was some kind of quiz-kid genius. The locus, victims, and moral onus of the deception have merely shifted ground over the intervening thirty-odd years.

Part 5

A

Comparative

Analysis

Chapter 17
The Price is Right Versus *Supermarket Sweep*

Revival

Despite the hegemony of the dominant ideology preached implicitly and displayed overtly by *The Price Is Right*—which is, as Bob Barker himself likes to remind us, the preeminent daytime network game show in terms of audience popularity (Landis)—we should not forget that other somewhat more wholesome examples of the genre do exist. In this connection, I would especially call attention to a program entitled *Supermarket Sweep*—originally broadcast on ABC from 1965 to 1967 and recently revived for broadcast over the Lifetime cable-television channel—which, according to Rimer, "calls itself the women's network" (D9). (For historical details, see Schwartz, Ryan, and Wostbrock 432.) In my reading, when compared with *The Price Is Right* (*PIR*), the show called *Supermarket Sweep* (*SS*) affords an illuminating study in contrasts.

Comparison

Compared with *PIR*, *SS* goes even further in the direction of valorizing consumption (as opposed to mere ownership) by celebrating the skills required for consumer behavior in general and demonstrated by shopping activities in particular. The announcer Johnny Gilbert introduces the program with the promise, "Welcome to the first supermarket in the world that gives you money." But he quickly follows with an assertion of the skill-oriented values that underlie this particular game show: "The whole idea is to shop smarter and faster than the next person."

Whereas *PIR* takes place in a lavish carnivalesque, casino-like atmosphere of Las Vegas-styled flashing lights, sparkling decorations, and glitter-covered gambling wheels, *SS* is staged in an actual supermarket—thereby reviving a thematic shopping-related venue that has appeared in game shows off and on since the mid-1940s (DeLong 127). Unlike Bob Barker on *PIR*, the young master of ceremonies David Ruprecht on *SS* wears informal clothing and stands in front of a down-to-earth produce display. In contrast to *PIR*'s Barker, this places *SS*'s Ruprecht on an elevational and visual par with the three sets of two contestants who generally wear comfortable but stylish garb (not sloppy), who are invariably young to middle aged (not older), who discuss their careers and lives in ways that reveal them to be attractive and intelligent (not depersonalized), and who stand in front of the soft-drink section near an end-of-aisle coffee display (not beneath the level of the M.C.).

By contrast with the often contemptuous putdowns offered by *PIR*'s Bob Barker, *SS*'s host David Ruprecht respectfully engages the contestants in conversations about their families, jobs, and lives in general. Often, the *SS* contestants turn out to be mother-and-daughter teams with interesting vocations, unmarried couples with exciting jobs, husbands and wives with professional careers, or graduate students at USC or UCLA. Throughout, unlike the contestants on *PIR* (who pursue self-interest based on luck), the visitors to *SS* display what often strikes me as close teamwork and remarkable skill in their knowledge of advertising slogans, their memory for brand names, their cognitive maps of the supermarket shelves, and their speed plus agility in manipulating the unwieldy shopping carts under time pressure.

In short, whereas *The Price Is Right* a focuses on materialism and an ethos of greed, *Supermarket Sweep* valorizes the consumption skills that intelligent, attractive, and knowledgeable consumers really do possess as they engage in their consuming activities. These differences may be summarized by the set of homologies shown in Table 1. [For a review of the importance attached to binary oppositions in the work of Lévi-Strauss, see Fiske (*Introduction* 116-117, 125-126, 131-132).]

TABLE 1

A Comparison Based on Key Homologies:
The Price is Right Versus *Supermarket Sweep*

	The Price Is Right	*Supermarket Sweep*
Master of Ceremonies		
Age	Old	Young
Dress	Formal	Informal
Position	Elevated	Down-to Earth
Attitude	Contemptuous	Respectful
Context		
Setting	Carnival/Casino	Supermarket
Budget	Lavish	Modest
Focus	Materialism	Consumption
Ethos	Greed	Skill
Contestants		
Age	Older	Younger
Dress	Sloppy	Casual
Personal lives	Depersonalized	Interesting
Motivation	Self-interest	Teamwork
Key factor	Luck	Talent

Three Stages

Supermarket Sweep proceeds in three stages. I shall describe each briefly.

Stage One

First, the two-person teams of contestants compete for

time in ten-second increments. They win time units by answering difficult consumption-related questions (often under pressure from the clock). For example, they might be asked to identify which of three items does not cost $1.17: (1) a 15-ounce can of Chef Boyardee Ravioli, (2) a 10.5-ounce can of Franco-American Turkey Gravy, or (3) a 19-ounce can of Progresso Lentil Soup (Answer: The turkey gravy). Or they might be asked to answer a riddle of the following form: "When Snap and Pop want some candy, they're obviously missing _____?" (Answer: Crackle); "If you've got bad breath, don't lose all hope; just reach for the product called _____" (Answer: Scope); or "For breath that is always fresh and clean, just keep on chewing the red-and-white package of _____" (Answer: Dentine). Or they might be asked to indicate which companies have the following spokespersons: Ernie the Elf, Elsie the Cow, an overweight white giggling baker, and Little Sprout (Answers: Keebler, Borden, Pillsbury, and Green Giant). Clearly, answering these sorts of questions demands a highly developed sense of prices, an awareness of company logos, and a recall of advertising jingles.

Stage Two

The second stage of *Supermarket Sweep* sends one member of each team into the market on a "sweep" in which contestants use the time they have won in the first stage to try to cram merchandise of the greatest possible value into their shopping carts. En route through the aisles, they may pick up bonus items worth from $50 to $200. They may also try to win a bonus of $250 by finding the three items on the *Supermarket Sweep* Shopping List for that day—for example, Glad Klingwrap, Raisinets, and Contac; Hungry Jack Mashed Potatoes, Rave Hair Spray, and Nacho Cheese Doritos; or Quaker Chewy Granola Bars, Louis Rich Lunch Breaks, and Stouffer's Frozen Chicken Pie. This challenging task sends the three contestants racing through the aisles, careening around corners with their overloaded shopping carts, diving for high-priced items (meats, hams, cheeses, salamis, health and beauty aids, family-sized boxes of detergent, paper diapers, garbage cans, hardware items) that they pass on the shelves (with a limit of five items per category to each customer), clutching at bonus-labeled end-of-aisle displays, and desperately trying to remember, find, and grab the three all-important Shopping-List items.

Meanwhile, the veteran game-show announcer Johnny Gilbert provides a running action-packed play-by-play account, as follows:

And there goes Marcia, smiling all the way. And she makes our famous left turn right to the meat counter. Now there goes Barbie of Team 2, and she has a different idea...with the detergent and lifting in those giant boxes of Surf—while Marcia is perking right along in the coffee section, and helping herself to those big three-pound cans, and she's about to help herself to a Shopping-List item; it's the Chung King Egg Rolls. But she's so excited, she passed a bonus. Did you see that? And Cynthia gets off to a screaming start. Must be her way of saying "Get out of my way." Sure, that's because she wants those steaks in our meat department....

At the end of the Sweep, the shoppers return to the checkout counters, where the total value of their groceries plus bonuses is computed. As they stand in front of the cut-flowers section, their totals are announced. The team with the highest total wins the right to compete for $5,000 in the third stage.

Stage Three

Stage Three involves solving three puzzles and finding the appropriate merchandise within a time limit of 60 seconds. Specifically, the two-person team of contestants must figure out the answer to the first clue, rush to the relevant brand in the supermarket, read the second clue, find the next target product, read the third clue, and find the third designated item —all in under one minute.

Two illustrative sets of three clues are as follows:

When your dirty child gets into *trouble*, put him in the tub with ___ _____? (Answer: Mr. Bubble); Cartoon character Fudd sticks to this product: _____ ____ (Answer: Elmer's Glue); Think of Sinbad the Sailor, sailing in the breeze, when you open a bottle of _____ ____? (Answer: Seven Seas).

If fruit is too tart it can make your lips *pucker*, but the *fruit* is always sweet in a jar named _____ (Answer: Smucker); If your puppy is getting chubby, let him ride on our exer-_____ (Answer: Cycle); It sounds like this spicy brown spread might be a favorite of actor Elliot _____ (Answer: Gulden's Mustard).

Clearly, the mental agility and physical dexterity required to solve these clues and rush to the appropriate locations in the market—not once, not twice, but three times—place some fairly extraordinary demands on the skills of the contestants. Yet the teams often manage to accomplish this remarkable feat. Indeed, on two or three occasions, I have seen them complete the task with as much as 20 seconds to spare.

Darkness and Light

In sum, if *The Price Is Right* represents the dark, insidious side of the game-show mystique, *Supermarket Sweep* appears to offer the contrapositive viewpoint from the perspective of sweetness and light. On *The Price Is Right*, contestants are rewarded for passively making lucky guesses or accidentally spinning a winning number. On *Supermarket Sweep*, the winners must demonstrate real consumer expertise, knowledge of prices, and shopping skill. The first program celebrates materialistic ownership; the second honors consumption.

Hegemony Revisited

Nevertheless, despite these noteworthy differences in outlook and tact, both programs appear to perform a similar function in terms of the dominant ideology behind the hegemonic ethos of the consumer society. Specifically, whether they be shady or sunny in their disposition, consumer-oriented game shows like *The Price Is Right* and *Supermarket Sweep* seem to play a signal role in the contemporary culture of consumption. However positive and gentle its viewpoint, *Supermarket Sweep* still invites an interpretation focusing on "the struggle for commodities as an epic combat of clashing trolleys" (Conrad 105).

Symbolically, then, both *The Price Is Right* and *Supermarket Sweep* reflect the obsession that many modern consumers feel with merchandise valued almost for its own sake, beyond any need or even capacity to use it, as a kind of disembodied target of desire. Disquietingly, both programs impose a frivolous but venal gaming mentality on consumption activities that in many parts of the world would inspire careful planning and involve problematic allocations of scarce resources. Disturbingly, both seem to justify a way of life in which material consumption is the target of existence. Collectively, with the other game shows, they legitimate an ethos in which Good Consumers are rewarded by Big Prizes.

After mopping the floor, one gets to splash in the hot tub. After bathing the baby, one gets to play with the home gym. And—ultimately, after one has paid one's dues by completing enough household chores or by sweeping through enough supermarkets—one may win the $5,000 or carry off the Whole Showcase in a blissful orgy of consumption in which, whatever the price one must pay, The Price Is Right.

Part 6

Epilogue

Chapter 18
Envoi

Yet I am left with one final troubling but strangely reassuring thought:

★ If game shows like *The Price Is Right* and *Supermarket Sweep* are primarily Exercises in Acquisitiveness, Monuments to Mammon, or Celebrations of Merchandise (and they are);

★ if they espouse values that reflect a capitalist ethic of materialism based on greed (and they do);

★ and if we should oppose such exaggerated examples of the culture of consumption gone berserk (and we should);

❤ then *why*—when the happy contestant on *The Price Is Right* wins the boat, the car, and the travel trailer; loses control; and begins jumping around the stage emitting hysterical shrieks of ecstasy;

❤ and *why*—when the frantic team on *Supermarket Sweep* successfully solves that third clue; rushes to the appropriate brand halfway down the second aisle on the left; and triumphantly locates the hidden bundle of prize money;

❤ yes, *why* do I so often find myself sitting there,

● helplessly grinning with a soaring sense of vicarious elation,

● laughing out loud despite myself, and

● rejoicing in my feeling of shared triumph?

115

Part 7

References

Works Cited

Allen, Robert C, ed. "Reader-Oriented Criticism and Television." *Channels of Discourse: Television and Contemporary Culture*. Chapel Hill: U of North Carolina, 1987.

Althusser, Louis. *Lenin and Philosophy*. Trans. Ben Brewster. New York: Monthly Review, 1971.

Altman, Rick. "Television Sound." Modleski *Studies in Entertainment*.

Ang, Ien. "Melodramatic Identifications: Television Fiction and Women's Fantasy." Brown *Television and Women's Culture*.

Angus, Ian and Sut Jhally, eds. *Cultural Politics in Contemporary America*. New York, NY: Routledge, 1989.

Arnold, Matthew. *Culture and Anarchy*. Ed. J. Dover Wilson, Cambridge: Cambridge UP, 1869, ed. 1932.

Barnouw, Eric. *Tube of Plenty: The Evolution of American Television*. New York, NY: Oxford UP, 1975.

_____. *Tube of Plenty: The Evolution of American Television*. 2nd rev. ed. New York, NY: Oxford UP, 1990.

Barthes, Roland. *Mythologies*. Trans. Annette Lavers. New York: Hill and Wang, 1972.

_____. *S/Z*. Trans. Richard Miller. New York: Hill and Wang, 1974.

Baudrillard, Jean. *America*. Trans. Chris Turner, London: Verso, 1989.

_____. *Cool Memories*. Trans. Chris Turner, London: Verso, 1990.

_____. *De la Séduction*. Paris: Editions Galilée, 1979. Partially repr. in Poster *Selected Writings*.

_____. *For a Critique of the Political Economy of the Sign*. Trans. Charles Levin, St. Louis, MO: Telos P, 1972. Partially repr. in Poster *Selected Writings*.

_____. *La Société de Consommation*. Paris: Gallimard, 1970. Partially repr. in Poster *Selected Writings*.

_____. *L'Échange Symbolique et la Mort*. Paris: Gallimard, 1976. Partially repr. in Poster *Selected Writings*.

_____. *Simulations*. Trans. Paul Foss, Paul Patton, and Philip Beitchman. New York, NY: Semiotext(e), 1983.

_____. *Le Systém des Objets*. Paris: Gallimard, 1968. Partially repr. in Poster *Selected Writings*.

_____. "The Ecstasy of Communication." Foster.

_____. *The Ecstasy of Communication*. Trans. Bernard Schutze and Caroline Schutze. Ed. Slyvere Lotringer, New York, NY: Semiotext(e), 1988.

Berger, Arthur Asa. *Media Analysis Techniques*. Rev. ed. Newbury Park, CA: Sage Publications, 1991.

Boddy, William. "The Seven Dwarfs and the Money Grubbers: The Public Relations Crisis of US Television in the Late 1950s." Mellencamp *Logics of Television*.

Brown, Mary Ellen, ed. "Conclusion: Consumption and Resistance—The Problem of Pleasure." *Television and Women's Culture: The Politics of the Popular*. London: Sage Publications, 1990.

_____. "Introduction: Feminist Cultural Television Criticism—Culture, Theory and Practice." *Television and Women's Culture*.

_____. "Motley Moments: Soap Operas, Carnival, Gossip and the Power of the Utterance." *Television and Women's Culture*.

Browne, Ray and Marshall Fishwick. *Icons of America*. Bowling Green, OH: Bowling Green State University Popular Press, 1978.

Brunt, Rosalind. "What's My Line?"*Television Mythologies: Stars, Shows & Signs*, ed. Len Masterman, London: Comedia Publishing Group/MK Media P, 21-28.

Brunsdon, Charlotte. "*Crossroads*: Notes on Soap Opera." Kaplan *Regarding Television*.

_____. "Television: Aesthetics and Audiences." Mellencamp *Logics of Television*.

Buckley, Tom. "Game Shows—TV's Glittering Gold Mine." *The New York Times Magazine* 18 Nov. 1979.

Caughie, John. "Playing at Being American: Games and Tactics," in *Logics of Television: Essays in Cultural Criticism,* ed. Patricia Mellencamp, Bloomington: Indiana UP, 44-58.

Chambers, Iain. *Popular Culture: The Metropolitan Experience*. London: Routledge, 1986.

Chun, Young H. "Game Show Problem." *OR/MS Today* June 1991.

Clark, Danae. "*Cagney & Lacey*: Feminist Strategies of Detection." Brown *Television and Women's Culture*.

Clark, Kenneth R. "Bob Barker: Host with Most Gamesmanship."

Chicago Tribune, TV Week, 3, 22 July 1990.

Comstock, George. *Television in America*. Beverly Hills, CA: Sage Publications, 1980.

Comstock, George, Steven Chaffee, Natan Katzman, Maxwell McCombs, and Donald Roberts. *Television and Human Behavior*. New York: Columbia UP, 1978.

Conrad, Peter. *Television: The Medium and Its Manners*. Boston: Routledge & Kegan Paul, 1982.

Corry, John. "In Shopping Games, the Bargain Is All." *New York Times*, C26, 8 July 1987.

DeLong, Thomas A. *Quiz Craze: America's Infatuation With Game Shows*. New York, NY: Praeger, 1991.

Deming, Caren J. "For Television-Centred Television Criticism: Lessons from Feminism." Brown *Television and Women's Culture*.

Eco, Umberto. *The Role of the Reader: Explorations in the Semiotics of Texts*. Bloomington: Indiana UP, 1979.

Enzenberger, Hans Magnus. *The Consciousness Industry*. New York, NY: Seabury, 1974.

Fabe, Maxine. *TV Game Shows*. Garden City, NY: Dolphin Books, 1979.

Feur, Jane. "Genre Study and Television." Allen *Channels of Discourse*.

Fishwick, Marshall W. *Parameters: Man-Media Mosaic*. Bowling Green, OH: Bowling Green State University Popular Press, 1978.

Fiske, John. "British Cultural Studies and Television." Allen.

_____. *Introduction to Communication Studies*. 2nd. ed. London: Routledge, 1990.

_____. *Television Culture*. London: Routledge, 1987.

_____. "Women and Quiz Shows: Consumerism, Patriarchy and Resisting Pleasures." Brown *Television and Women's Culture*.

Fiske, John and John Hartley. *Reading Television*. London: Methuen, 1978.

Flitterman, Sandy. "*The Real* Soap Operas: TV Commercials." Kaplan *Regarding Television*.

Foster, Hal, ed. *The Anti-Aesthetic: Essays on Postmodern Culture*. Seattle, WA: Bay, 1983.

Fowles, Jib. *Television Viewers Vs. Media Snobs*. New York, NY: Stein and Day, 1982.

Gans, Herbert J. *Popular Culture and High Culture: An Analysis and Evaluation of Taste*. New York: Basic Books, 1974.

Gendron, Bernard. "Theodor Adorno Meets the Cadillacs." Modleski *Studies in Entertainment*.

Gitlin, Todd. *Inside Prime Time*. New York: Pantheon Books, 1983.

_____. The *Whole World Is Watching: Mass Media in the Making & Unmaking of the New Left*. Berkeley, CA: U of California P, 1980.

Good, Leslie T. "Power, Hegemony, and Communication Theory." Angus and Jhally *Culture Politics*.

Goodbody, Jerry. "America's Vanishing Housewife." *Adweek's Marketing Week* 32 (26), 24 June 1991.

Goodman, Walter. "For $64,000: Who Lost in the Big Fix?" *The New York Times*, (5 January 1992), H31.

Gottdiener, M. "Hegemony and Mass Culture: A Semiotic Approach." *American Journal of Sociology*, 90 (March 1985).

Gramsci, Antonio,*Selections from the Prison Notebooks of Antonio Gramsci*. Ed. Quintin Hoare and Geoffrey Nowell-Smith. New York, NY: International Publishers, 1971.

Hall, Stuart. "Encoding/Decoding." *Culture, Media, Language*. Ed. S. Hall, D. Hobson, A. Lowe, and P. Willis. London: Hutchinson, 1980.

Heath, Stephen. "Representing Television." Mellencamp *Logics of Television*.

Heath, Stephen and Gillian Skirrow. "An Interview With Raymond Williams." Modleski *Studies in Entertainment*.

Hebdige, Dick. *Subculture: The Meaning of Style*. New York: Methuen, 1979.

Hebdige, Dick. *Hiding in the Light*. London: Comedia, 1987.

Hickey, Neil. "What Do You Mean It's Only a Game?" *Television Today: A Close-Up View*. Ed. Barry Cole, New York: Oxford UP, 1981.

How to Use PRIZM. Alexandria, VA: Claritas Corporation, 1986.

Huyssen, Andreas. "Mass Culture As Woman: Modernism's Other." Modleski *Studies in Entertainment*.

Jameson, Fredric. "Postmodernism and Consumer Society." Foster *The Anti-Aesthetic*.

_____. *The Political Unconscious: Narrative As a Socially Symbolic Act*. Ithaca, NY: Cornell UP, 1981 *Cultural Politics*.

Jhally, Sut. "Advertising as Religion: The Dialectic of Technology and Magic." Angus and Jhally *Cultural Politics.*

_____. "The Political Economy of Culture." Angus and Jhally *Cultural Politics.*

Kaplan, E. Ann. "Feminist Criticism and Television." Allen *Channel of Discourse.*

Kaplan, E. Ann, ed. "Introduction." *Regarding Television: Critical Approaches—An Anthology.* Frederick, MD: University Publications of America, 1983.

Kilbourne, William E. "Self-Actualization and the Consumption Process: Can You Get There From Here?" *Philosophical and Radical Thought in Marketing.* Eds. A. Fuat Firat, Nikhilesh Dholakia, and Richard P. Bagozzi. Lexington, MA: Lexington Books, 1987.

King, Susan. "Bob Barker Wins the Game of Endurance." *Los Angeles Times.* TV Times, 2 (8 July 1990).

Kozloff, Sarah Ruth. "Narrative Theory and Television." Allen *Channels of Discourse.*

Landis, David. "Soap Sweep." *USA Today* 21 June 1991.

Larrain, Jorge. "Stuart Hall and the Marxist Concept of Ideology." *Theory, Culture & Society* 8 November 1991.

Lazere, Donald. "Mass Culture, Political Consciousness and English Studies." *College English* 38 April 1977.

"Letters—Goats Vs. Cars II: The War Continues." *OR/MS Today* 18 August 1991.

Lévi-Strauss, Claude. *The Raw and the Cooked.* London: Cape, 1969.

Lewis, Bill. "TV Games: People as Performers." *Television Mythologies: Stars, Shows & Signs.* Ed. Len Masterman, London: Comedia Publishing Group, 1984.

Lewis, Lisa A. "Consumer Girl Culture: How Music Video Appeals to Girls," Brown *Television and Women's Culture.*

Lopate, Carol. "Day-Time Television: You'll Never Want to Leave Home." *Feminist Studies,* 4 (6), 1976.

Macdonald, Dwight. *Against the American Grain.* New York: Da Capo, 1962.

Marchetti, Gina. "Action-Adventure as Ideology." *Cultural Politics in Contemporary America.* Angus and Jhally *Cultural Politics.*

Masterman, Len, ed. "Introduction." *Television Mythologies: Stars, Shows & Signs.* London: Comedia Publishing Group, 1984.

Matelski, Marilyn J. and David O. Thomas. *Variety Broadcast-*

Video Sourcebook I: 1989-1990. Boston: Focal, 1990.

McArthur, Colin. "TV Commercials: Moving Statues and Old Movies." Masterman *Television Mythologies*.

McQuail, D., J. Blumler, and R. Brown. "The Television Audience: A Revised Perspective." *Sociology of Mass Communications*. Ed. D. McQuail, Harmondsworth: Penguin, 1972.

Mellencamp, Patricia. "Prologue." *Logics of Television: Essays in Cultural Criticism*. Bloomington: Indiana UP, 1990.

_____. "Situation Comedy, Feminism, and Freud: Discourses of Gracie and Lucy." Modleski *Studies in Entertainment*.

Modleski, Tania, ed. "Introduction." *Studies in Entertainment: Critical Approaches to Mass Culture*. Bloomington, IN: Indiana UP, 1986.

Modleski, Tania. "The Rhythms of Reception: Daytime Television and Women's Work." Kaplan *Regarding Television*.

Morley, David. *Family Television: Cultural Power and Domestic Leisure*. London: A Comedia Book, 1986.

Morris, Margaret. "Banality in Cultural Studies." Mellencamp *Logics of Television*.

Morse, Margaret. "Sport on Television: Replay and Display." Kaplan *Regarding Television*.

Muntean, Greg and Gregg Silverman. *How to Become a Game Show Contestant: An Insider's Guide*. New York, NY: Fawcett Columbine, 1987.

Nightingale, Virginia. "Women as Audiences." Brown *Television and Women's Culture*.

Polan, Dana. "Brief Encounters: Mass Culture and the Evacuation of Sense." Modleski *Studies in Entertainment*.

Poster, Mark, ed. *Selected Writings;Jean Baudrillard*. Stanford, CA: Stanford UP, 1988.

Press, Andrea L. "Class, Gender and the Female Viewer: Women's Responses to *Dynasty*." Brown *Television and Women's Culture*.

_____. *Women Watching Television: Gender, Class, and Generation in the American Television Experience*. Philadelphia, PA: U of Pennsylvania P, 1991.

Rapping, Elayne. *The Looking Glass World of Nonfiction TV*. Boston, MA: South End, 1987.

Ricoeur, Paul. *Interpretation Theory: Discourse and the Surplus of Meaning*. Fort Worth, TX: The Texas Christian UP, 1976.

Rimer, Sara. "TV Just for Women...and Men." *The New York*

Times 11 Nov. 1991.

Said, Edward W. "Opponents, Audiences, Constituencies and Community." Foster *The Anti-Aesthetic*.

Schroeder, Fred E. H. *Outlaw Aesthetics: Arts and the Public Mind*. Bowling Green, OH: Bowling Green State University Popular Press, 1977.

Schwartz, David, Steve Ryan, and Fred Wostbrock. *The Encyclopedia of TV Game Shows*. New York: Zoetrope, 1987.

Seiter, Ellen. "Semiotics and Television." Allen *Channels of Discourse*.

Skornia, Harry J. *Television and Society: An Inquest and Agenda for Improvement*. New York: McGraw-Hill Book Company, 1965.

Stam, Robert. "Television News and Its Spectator." Kaplan *Regarding Television*.

Stockbridge, Sally. "Rock Video: Pleasure and Resistance," Brown *Television and Women's Culture*.

Tetzlaff, David. "Divide and Conquer: Popular Culture and Social Control in Late Capitalism." *Media, Culture and Society*. 13 Jan. 1991.

Tierney, John. "Behind Monty Hall's Doors: Puzzle, Debate and Answer?" *The New York Times* 21 July 1991.

Trebek, Alex and Peter Barsocchini. *The JEOPARDY! Book: The Answers, the Questions, the Facts, and the Stories of the Greatest Game Show in History*. New York, NY: Harper Perennial, 1990.

Wayda, Stephen. "Dian Parkinson, Come On Down!" *Playboy*. 38 Dec. 1991.

White, Mimi. "Ideological Analysis and Television." Allen *Channels of Discourse*.

Williams, Raymond. *Marxism and Literature*. Oxford: Oxford UP, 1977.

_____. *Television: Technology and Cultural Form*. New York: Schocken Books, 1975.

Williamson, Judith. "Woman Is an Island: Femininity and Colonization." Modleski *Studies in Entertainment*.